DEDICATION

This book is for my daughter, Samantha. It's also dedicated to the memory of Coach Jack Pack, who, along with his wife Sue, taught me a great deal about working with young people by helping me when I was young.

HOW TO USE THIS BOOK

I put this before the table of contents on purpose to get you to think about what you want out of this book and give you my suggestions about how to best use it.

Here are your options for reading this book:

1. **Don't.** A lot of you probably got this as a gift, and, after you shook the book to loose any gift card or cash that may be stuck in there, what's the point? Well, if you're reading this then you're at least marginally interested in what the book is about. Certainly, you want to graduate in four years, but you're not sure if this book will help you. You're also not sure if you need help at all.

    I don't know you, so I don't know what you need. But I do know a lot of students who are probably somewhat like you. And I've written this book somewhat differently than most college guides or self-help books. I viewed my job as getting you to think about what's best for you, while also helping you with the practical and logistical hoops you have jump through to graduate college in four years.

    If you don't want to read the book, don't. But look at the chapter titles in the table of contents and keep the book. At some point, the book will probably come in handy.

2. **Read Some Selected Chapters.** I would read the chapters at the beginning of each section; you can tell what they are by looking at the table of contents. In addition to those, I'd read the chapters *Student Loans*; *Meeting People*; *Eat, Sleep, & Exercise*; *Set Goals*; *Mental Health*; *Learn to Learn*; *Majors*; and *Advising*. That's less than a third of the book, and it's not a very long book.

I organized the book topically to make it easy to use just what you need, when you need it.

3. **Read the Whole Thing.** I'd love it if you read the whole book. Please drop me an email if you do because I'll be super flattered. I do think reading the whole book has one distinct advantage: we often don't know what we don't know. You may have some pretty important questions that you don't even know you have.

Contact Me

I love to talk to students and their families. I don't charge to answer questions, and it's always a thrill to hear from readers.

If you found a typo, disagree with something in the book, or think I'm missing some important topic, please let me know. While this book is my baby (except for my real baby), I want it to be as good as it can be, and you'll be doing me a favor by pointing out where I come up short.

I also offer academic coaching for college students, standardized test prep (ACT, SAT, GRE, GMAT, & LSAT), and help with college and graduate/professional school admissions. I can be reached through my website, www.thetestguy.com, or you can email me directly at Jacob@thetestguy.com.

Table of Contents

GRADUATE IN FOUR YEARS

If you read the back cover of this book, you may recall that I wrote, "Surviving college is insufficient." I may have partially borrowed that line from a science fiction novel, but I couldn't believe the sentiment any more strongly.

This book appears to have two goals: to get you to a cap and gown in four years and to have you leave that graduation ceremony a happy, healthy adult with plenty of opportunities, confidence, and faith in your future.

In reality, those aren't different goals. My goal is to get you to realize that how you live and what you do are not separate nor are they separable. My goal is to get you to approach life with intentionality, to plan, to persist, to pursue. I want you to learn how to make smart trades with your time, effort, and attention. And I want you to learn that success is a matter of consistent effort more than any "fixed" talent or ability.

College sets the tone for adulthood. How you eat, sleep, use substances, exercise, treat others, respond to pressure, interact with peers and superiors, and manage your workload will not change as soon as you are handed a diploma. There are as many ways to build a happy and successful life as there are people, but, those lives all have some similarities. I've tried to distill what I consider those similarities into actionable, customizable advice.

From a practical standpoint, **let's talk about what needs to happen for you to graduate in four years**:

1. **You need to take and pass the equivalent of 15 hours (or equivalent) per semester.** It takes 120 hours—or thereabouts—to graduate; broken down into 8 semesters that equates 15 hours a semester.

2. **You have to be a smart consumer.** Don't expect your adviser to always have the answer or predict your needs. You need to make a plan for how to get through your major classes and the general education requirements at your college (check out the chapters on *Majors* & *General Education requirements* for more). Watch out for bottlenecks in prerequisites or major courses. Anticipate difficulty down the line and leave yourself some wiggle room to graduate. A fragile plan is no plan at all.

3. **You have put in effort daily.** All-nighters and last-ditch efforts are a lot more romantic in movies than they are in real life. If you want to do more than survive college, you need to be productive every day. Not only will your grades be better, but you'll have more opportunities, be less stressed, and have more time for fun.

4. **You have to provide your own structure.** A big part of being an adult is doing things when no one is making you. The freedoms of college are great, but those freedoms are matched with responsibilities. You can wing it, and it may work out for you. But I promise you, as someone who has tried it both ways, you'll be happier if you create a structured life for yourself.

5. **You have to be happy.** I'm not joking about this. I know the first half of this list has been a bit of a downer, but here's the deal: you can't avoid work. You just can't. So, structure your life so work is easier, less stressful, and balanced with fun and new experiences. Even if you're the most introverted of introverts, you need friends, you need passions, and you need new experiences.

6. **You have to take care of yourself.** Still not joking. Eating terribly and not exercising is part of the college identity, but you'll be healthier, happier, and feel better if you make reasonable choices. You don't have to be a health nut or a gym rat, but it's important to find a balance. You also need to take care of your mental health; **more than half of you will have a mental health crisis in college**. Please read the chapter on *Mental Health*.

7. **You have to be working towards something.** Graduating college in four years is *a* goal, not the goal. You need to think beyond college, what kind of work do you want to do? Do you want to go to graduate or professional school? You'll want to make those decisions at some point before you graduate, and, in general, earlier is better. (Don't ever feel locked in though, you can always change your mind).

You need goals, and if you have no idea what you want to do, figuring that out is your first step. I once thought goal setting was dumb, but I've found it's made my life much richer. It's easier to work hard when you see it as part of an overarching objective.

Why Students Don't Graduate in Four Years

The worst end to your college experience is dropping out with a ton of debt and no better off in the employment market. The second worst outcome is graduating with a ton of debt and low earnings potential. Graduating in four years is crucial to giving you the freedom to choose what sort of work you do while being able to create a stable financial life. The longer you take to graduate, the fewer employment and graduate/professional school options you have. You'll also have fewer options over what jobs you can afford to take.

1. **Transferring.** Transferring almost always costs some or even all of your hours. It's a very serious decision to transfer, and all too often students are transferring because of issues that won't be fixed by changing colleges. Please check out the chapter on *Transferring Colleges* for more.

2. **Not taking enough hours.** 12 hours a semester is full-time, but you won't graduate in four years that way. Take 15 a semester to finish on time.

3. **Not planning and organizing.** You need your own roadmap to graduation, otherwise you could be stuck behind a prerequisite or not be able to get into a required course and end up hanging around for the summer, a semester, or even a year to chase a few hours. Check out the chapters *Advising*, *Majors*, and *General Education* for more.

4. **Working too much.** Working more than 20 hours a week is negatively correlated with GPA, time to graduation, and graduation rates. It's almost impossible to work your way through

school, wages are low and tuition is high. If you're working because it makes you "more responsible" your time would be better spent in internships and campus involvement. For many non-traditional students, not working is not an option. I suggest you check out the *Grants* chapter of this book, as you may be able to find enough grant money to reduce the number of hours you work.

5. **Being unhappy.** Your concentration suffers, your drive suffers, your work suffers. It's hard to make goals, and it's hard to follow through. If you aren't happy, you can never truly thrive. Check out the chapters *Meet People*, *Get Involved*, and *Mental Health* for help.

6. **Being unhealthy.** if you are physically or mentally unwell, everything suffers. You can't separate how you feel from how you do. Check out the chapters *Eat, Sleep, & Exercise*, and *Mental Health* for more.

7. **They don't seek accommodations for disability.** If you have a physical disability, learning disability or mental health condition, please seek accommodations. You don't have to use them if you choose not to. Check out the chapter *Accommodations for Disability* for more.

I hope you enjoy the book, and I hope it helps. If the ink isn't dry on your high school diploma yet, this is your life now. It's yours to do as much or as little as you choose. If you've been in college for awhile and you're reading this, you probably want to make a change. It's never too late to make a change, to start defining or redefining yourself. I've done it several times and I'm only 33. If you're a non-traditional student, I admire you. What you're doing is hard, and when it gets tough remind yourself of why you started.

1 BEFORE COLLEGE STARTS

I'm not going to spend much time discussing college selection. That's not what this book is about, but there's plenty written about it online and in print. I will, however, give you a few things that I think are tremendously important in selecting a college. I'll also give you a list of really bad reasons for selecting a college.

<u>Picking a College: Pick What's Important</u>

Everything in life is a tradeoff. When it comes to selecting a college, you'll make trades based on prestige, strength of program, financial aid, total cost, location, and personal preferences. It's really important that you think things through. What will life be like beyond college? How attached am I to this particular goal or idea of my future? What's the likelihood that this school can get me to where I want to be (provided I do my part)? For me, two questions are most important.

Can this college get me where I want to be? If you aren't sure, you should ask. Talk to people within a department, career services, and at professional schools. If possible, find statistics for graduate admissions and employment rates.

Is it worth the cost? If a school is more expensive—after financial aid—make sure the extra money is well spent. Do you get a significant bump in prestige, opportunities, or education? <u>One thing about cost, don't hesitate to apply to schools that have a higher cost. It's impossible to tell what financial aid the school will come back with—most students do not pay the full price.</u>

Picking a College: What's Not Important

You may not believe me now, but trust me the following are not important considerations.

But my boyfriend (girlfriend) – I really wish there were statistics available on what percentage of high school relationships last through college. There aren't (and I really, really looked). In my experience, working with over a thousand students over the years, it's almost nil. As someone who, as an adult, made a significant life decision for a significant other that I wouldn't have had otherwise, and then had that relationship end, I can tell you it is not fun. Make your own decision. Don't think about the boy or girlfriend. If it's a strong, healthy relationship, it will work.

But my friends – The world has so many fascinating people in it. Your friends will stay your friends or not. In my experience, one of two things happens when you go to college with friends. You either end up spending way too much time with your high school friends and limiting the people you meet in college, thereby diminishing your college experience. Or, you end up not spending much time with those people at all because you've made new friends. **You are about to change a lot.** So are they.

When people want to go to college with their friends, it's usually because they're afraid. Afraid they won't meet anyone they like, afraid no one will care about them, afraid they won't find anyone that fills the emotional needs their friends do.

There's absolutely nothing wrong with being afraid. But the first (and best) step to getting over fear is acknowledging that it exists. You haven't read much of this book yet, but one thing you may notice is that much of my advice is geared to getting you to think about what works for you in your situation. You're all incredibly different people with different needs, circumstances, abilities, and goals. It would be irresponsible of me to tell you exactly what to do, because that kind of advice is just telling you what I would do. I say all that to emphasize this point: **all of you can make some of the best friends you'll ever have in college. You don't need your friends from high school there to do it.**

But my family It's going to be hard to go away to school. Hard on you (even if you won't admit it) and hard on your family. You'll miss them and they will miss you. It's time to build your life, though. And that may keep you relatively close to where you grew up, or it may take you to another continent.

But my faith If you're religious, you have to live in the same world as the rest of us. Isolating yourself does you a disservice in your ability to interact with the world and pursue many careers. It's also very likely to turn you into a narrow minded and intolerant adult, unable to empathize with others.

I have very, very strong feelings about many of the evangelical colleges that operate in the United States. Particularly how they treat their students (especially young women) and the (low) quality of the education they provide. Those are, of course, my feelings but I'm leaving them in the book for a reason. **Never attend any college that is unaccredited, and be very careful about provisional accreditation.** Many students have been duped by colleges whose accreditation is "just right around the corner."

That said, going to a religious college is no guarantee of religiosity among students or faculty. Most Catholic colleges and universities don't have much of a traditional Catholic education. The same goes with protestant colleges and universities that are more mainstream. I'm not Christian, but I would be very happy if my daughter attended Notre Dame (Catholic), Baylor (Baptist), or studied creative writing at Brigham Young (Mormon).

There are a few high quality institutions who maintain a strong religious affiliation, Providence College and Lee University for example. For the most part, though, religious colleges are either religious in name only or they're part of a problematic, poorly operating fundamental group of colleges that persists throughout the US.

But my lack of faith – I doubt my daughter will be religious, neither her mother or I are and that's by far the strongest indicator. (I really don't care if she is religious, or what religion she would be, as long as she's a kind and generous person).

But if my daughter said she wouldn't consider Loyola or Villanova because of their religious affiliation, I would give her a talking to. Even if the college required some nominal religious participation, it wouldn't kill her. But, in reality, she would have marginally more contact with that faith than she would at a public or non-religious private university.

Do Not Attend a For-Profit University

My attorney and I have a bet; it's my contention that I won't get a cease and desist letter (or worse) from a for-profit college for the next paragraph. He thinks otherwise.

For profit colleges are a rip off. They provide a substandard education. They cost more and give you less. They make up statistics about job placement and salary. Your credits will probably not transfer. I have included a few articles in the Resources section below, but please research any for-profit or online only school. Don't take their "admissions counselors" or "academic counselors" at face value; they are almost always paid salespeople.

Resources

The Downfall or For-Profit Colleges Alia Wong	theatlantic.com/education/archive/2015/02/the-downfall-of-for-profit-colleges/385810/
For Profit Colleges New York Times	nytimes.com/topic/subject/forprofit-schools

2 ORIENTATION

What it's Like

Orientation feels long (even the short ones), it's much more structured than college itself, and it's information overload. But, colleges and universities spend a lot of time and resources on orientation, and you can get a lot out of it. Orientations vary quite a bit by college and your college may offer several options, ranging in length from half a day to several days. Within colleges, there may be different options for the length of your orientation and special orientations for majors, student athletes, and honors students.

What to Bring

It depends on the college. You may need vaccination records, documentation of disability, your birth certificate, and other official paperwork. Make sure you've read everything the college has sent you regarding the nuts and bolts of housing, financial aid, student policies, and registration. Put some thought into goal setting before orientation; it'll help you get into the right classes and set you up for success. Check out the chapter on *Goal Setting* for more.

What Goes Down

Advising & Registration – While I'm listing advising first, it's usually one of the last activities at orientation. You'll meet with your advisor for the first time. Depending on your college/university this will either be a faculty member or an advisor from the college's undergraduate advising center. In either case, be open with your adviser and explain your short and long term goals. It always pays to be an informed consumer, so check out the chapter on *Advising*, for details on how to deal with your advising appointment.

Campus Tour – You'll take a campus tour, either as a randomly sorted group or as a group sorted by department or major. If you've toured your college before, you'll find this tour to be more informative and practical and less about salesmanship. Pay attention to campus facilities like the fitness center, tutoring centers, writing labs, etc.

Lots of Speeches & Presentations – I won't lie, orientation kind of sucks. There are a litany of quasi-motivational talks given by the President, Provost, and sundry deans and Vice Presidents. That said, there's a fair amount of information dispensed. Pay attention as best you can. Try to get familiar with the school's services and policies as well as how you'd look up anything else you'd need to know.

Some Awkward Social Stuff – Think of this as a test run for starting school (check out the chapter on *Meeting People* for more). There may or may not be icebreaker games and the like. Regardless, say hello, be friendly and meet people. If your orientation is over multiple days, stay in the dorms. You'll meet people that way and have your evening(s) open to do what you'd like. There are evening activities, but they are usually optional, so feel free to go out with your new friends and do something else. If orientation seems really rocky, trust me meeting people is a lot easier once you move to campus.

Student Organizations will be Recruiting – Getting involved on campus is incredibly important (check out the *Getting Involved* chapter). The student organizations have booths or tables, and it's likely some of them will speak during orientation. Give them your new university email address, and they'll keep you informed as to what's going on and when. There's no obligation to join, but check a bunch out.

Get Your ID Picture Taken – It doesn't matter how your picture looks, but I know some of you will disagree. My Costco membership picture looks like a mugshot. That said, it doesn't hurt to look decent, you're meeting people for the first time and first impressions count.

All the Sudden it's Real – This is one of those moments where the enormity of the college experience can kick in. If you feel overwhelmed, remember your school is offering this to help you, you can always ask questions in the future if need be, and that everyone around you is in the same boat.

Orientation for Parents

The many colleges and universities offer orientation activities for parents. These activities are designed to help parents with their transition; I know it's hard to imagine, but you going to college is really hard for them. Parents generally find these activities worthwhile as it gives them a better sense of how the institution works and what your life will be like there. My mother has always said that she feels better once she sees the place I'm living in because then she can picture me there. I think there's something to that; it's good for parents to see that the institution cares about you, has resources available to help you, is invested in your success, and is a good place for you to grow.

3 PLACEMENT TESTS

College placement tests are meant to ensure take the right course. <u>If you've had a recent ACT/SAT score, you probably won't have to take a placement test unless you're trying to test out of a course</u>. Community colleges rely more on placement tests than four-year institutions, because their students have a wider variance in ability and they have more non-traditional students. Placement tests are most commonly used to judge readiness for math courses and English composition courses. Other placement tests can be used to test your science or foreign language knowledge.

The Uses of Placement Tests

Placement tests are used to move you back to a more introductory level, keep you the same, or move you forward to a more advanced course. Let's look at each case.

Move Back – Your placement test can be used to move you to a more elementary class. You could be moved from trig to college algebra, or from credited courses to uncredited courses. Many students end up taking a remedial English or mathematics course, and there's no shame in it. It's far more important to start college off on the right foot and have a good semester. Your college wants you to succeed, and they're doing this to try and help you.

Keep you the Same – Your placement test may indicate you should start with the traditional course, English 101 or College Algebra, for example.

Move you up – You may place into Calc. 1 or English 102, depending on your score. Cautionary note, discretion is the better part of valor. Don't necessarily take the hardest class you can if you *just barely* qualify for it, or if taking that course doesn't feel comfortable. Especially if the course is fundamental to your major.

What to Expect

The most common placement tests are the *Accuplacer*, by the College Board (SAT) and the *ACT Compass* by the ACT. Both are computer-based, multiple choice tests, but you'll have a pencil, paper, and a calculator as needed. The tests are computer adaptive, which means they adapt to how you're performing. Answer a question right, and your next question will be of equal or harder difficulty; answer a question wrong and you'll get an easier question.

Your Placement Depends on Your Score – Colleges will set their own cutoff scores for enrolling in courses. For example, you may need to get a 68 on the Compass Math Test to be able to enroll in college algebra.

Should I Prepare?

The test makers say no. They argue that tests should be taken as if you were walking into class the first day. Further, they allege that preparation won't necessarily improve scores.

I disagree, it's probably been awhile since you've had geometry, algebra, or a solid grammar review, so you're bound to be rusty. You're also unfamiliar with the test, which adds a layer of complexity for people who aren't great test takers. (When they discourage prep because it can skew results, it contradicts their argument that test prep doesn't affect results).

How Should I Prepare?

1. **Set a goal.** Ask your adviser/registration department what test they offer, and what the cutoffs are for the course you're aiming for. While you're at it, ask if they have a practice test or question set you can work (most don't, unfortunately).

2. **Work problems.** If your school has practice problems, great! If not, just google "Accuplacer practice problems" or "Compass practice problems." Each test has a few different formats, so be clear which one you are taking. In a pinch, you can practice with ACT/SAT prep questions. Check out the Resources section of this chapter for some links to Accuplacer and Compass practice problems.

3. **Review your weaknesses.** Spend some time on YouTube looking up explanatory videos. You'll find that you're not as hopeless as you think.

Subject Specific Placement Tests (Before College)

AP & IB Tests – A 3+ on the relevant AP test or a 4+ on the High Level IB exam will earn you credit at many colleges.

SAT II Subject Tests – The scoring for credit and placement varies for the SAT II, and the SAT II's aren't as popular as the AP/IB Exam series. Unless your school has competitive admissions, it may not even have a formal policy regarding turning a test score into credit and/or placement.

If you're being placed based on AP, IB, or SAT II scores, trust your own judgement. If you feel like you should be able to test out of a course, contact your college/university prior to enrolling.

Subject Specific Placement Tests (At Orientation/College)

Many colleges and universities design their own subject specific courses. For example, to test out of English 101, students may be required to write an essay about a pre-selected topic within a time limit. Never walk into a placement test cold; ask what the format of the test will be, as well as what material will be covered. Make sure you ask what successful students have done to prepare.

There are also companies who design and sell subject specific design (ALEKS.com is a major provider). If you're facing one of these tests, spend some time on google researching test taker experiences and practice questions.

Resources

Compass Practice Problems	act.org/content/dam/act/unsecured/documents/numerical.pdf
Accuplacer	accuplacer.collegeboard.org/sites/default/files/accuplacer-sample-questions-for-students.pdf

4 WHAT DOES COLLEGE REALLY COST?
Real Cost of Attendance, The FAFSA, & The CSS

The real cost of college is incredibly variable. There is also quite a bit of variability, just like any major purchase like a house or a car. The average tuition for a four-year public college/university is $9,410 in-state and $23,890 out-of-state. Private schools have an average tuition of $32,410. Add to that books (~$1,200 a year), room and board (an average of $8,887 at public colleges/universities and $10,089 at private colleges/universities). Then tack on a cell phone bill, clothing, supplies, and sundry expenses. In the resources section of this chapter you'll find a link to a page that has the cost for the average student at 1,550 colleges and universities.

Every college/university has a *net cost calculator*, which will give you an idea of how much you'll actually be paying. The school's net cost calculator may or may not work with out-of-state tuition, and they are designed for first-time freshmen (not transfers). Also, remember the calculators are based on current, or recent historical numbers, so they tend to underestimate.

These net cost calculators are involved, taking between 10 and 30 minutes to complete the inputs. You'll need your tax information on hand to be exact, although ballpark numbers are OK. It can be tricky to find your school's calculator (on purpose, in some cases); the resources section at the end of this chapter includes a link to 300 net price calculators at different institutions.

The net price quoted is the total cost of tuition and fees, room and board, and other student expenses *minus* the amount of federal aid the student is eligible for (not including Parent PLUS Loans and some grants). Most colleges now include scholarships in their calculator as well.

4

Over half of students decide whether to apply to a college based on the overall cost—the sticker price—of the school without considering what their family will be expected to pay or what that college costs for the average student. **Always have an idea of what your family is expected to contribute and what a college "really" costs.**

If You're Still Choosing Colleges / Thinking of Transferring

If you're still selecting your future alma mater, cost needs to be a top consideration. Check out the resources section for more on how to calculate costs and evaluate your options. Don't neglect any cost of living changes.

Remember, transferring often comes with a loss of some (or even all) credits. Before you commit to transferring, have a clear idea of what credits will and won't transfer. If transferring adds a semester or more to earning your degree, you may end up losing money in the long run, especially if you'll max out your low cost federal grants and loans.

Financial Aid

I'm going to keep the discussion of financial aid applications relatively short, because I'm assuming you're already fairly far down the path to starting college, or that you are already in college. If you check out the resources section of this chapter, I've included a link to a guide on financial aid that I really like.

To qualify for need-based and some merit-based financial aid (grants, scholarships, & loans), you'll have to fill out one of the major financial aid applications. There are two major applications: the FAFSA and the CSS.

The FAFSA is the Free Application for Federal Student Aid. The length and difficulty of the FAFSA is proportionate to how complicated your income, obligations, and assets are. Social security benefits, combat pay, and some retirement contributions count as income. Many of the inputs are pulled from your tax return, but you'll be asked additional questions about dependents, savings, and other assets. The FAFSA does not account for unsecured household debt (credit cards and previous student loans). Debt will **not** reduce what you're expected to pay for college.

If you're self-employed or you have quite a bit going on in your financial life, you may want to consider using an accountant. I generally tell families that if they couldn't do their taxes without an accountant, have your accountant complete the FAFSA.

Because the FAFSA is the application for federal aid, it's the most important, and you should fill one out, even if you expect to pay cash. Many merit based awards require a FAFSA, even if there is no need component.

The FAFSA will determine your Expected Family Contribution (check out the resources section of this chapter for a link to an EFC calculator). The EFC is the minimum you're expected to pay for your education, but use it as a loose estimate. Beyond your ability to qualify for federal aid, there's not a lot of concrete information given by your FAFSA. **As a rule of thumb, most colleges do not meet the entire EFC, unless they really want you to go to school there.**

Each college uses the FAFSA information in their own calculations.

File your FAFSA as early as possible. The FAFSA for the next school year opens on October 1 of the preceding year. For example, the FAFSA for 2018 – 2019 opened on October 1, 2017. You'll use the information from the taxes year before that. So, for the 2018 – 2019, you'd use your tax information from 2016.

Different states and schools have different FAFSA deadlines, but financial aid is first come, first served, and not all programs have unlimited funding. If you have a low EFC, it's doubly important to get the FAFSA in as soon as possible for programs like Perkins Loans (check the *Loans* chapter) and the FSEOG (check the *Grants* chapter).

You almost certainly will need to file a FASA to get scholarships from your college. These scholarships, particularly at higher tiers, have limited funding, so, again, file as soon as possible. Colleges are the single biggest dispenser of scholarship dollars; don't miss out.

If you've experienced a change in your financial situation, you can amend your FAFSA or provide more up-to-date data. You'll also want to talk to your college's financial aid office right away.

The CSS Profile is the College Scholarship Service offered by the College Board (the SAT people). Many of you will not need the CSS, and it's used far less frequently than the FAFSA. A few hundred colleges require it, however. By in large, the colleges that require the CSS are private institutions.

The CSS has an application fee of 25 dollars which can be waved for low-income students applying to college for the first time.

Filling out the CSS is a bit more involved. The CSS takes an hour or more to complete, and it will ask more detailed questions about any savings accounts, small business value, primary residence, private school tuition, and other assets. Divorced parents will have to fill out a separate Noncustodial PROFILE. The CSS has the advantage (if you live in an expensive area) of including the cost of living in your area.

The CSS has stricter deadlines. You can file the CSS as early as October 1, and you should make every effort to do so. Like the FAFSA, much aid is given on a first come, first served basis. **Every school has their own CSS deadline, but it's common for that deadline to be a few weeks <u>before</u> the early application/early decision deadline.**

<u>Living On-Campus vs. Off-Campus</u>

You can, theoretically, save money by living off campus. In practice, however, this isn't usually the case. Once you add utilities, internet, groceries, and so on, most students end up spending as much as they would in the dorms or more. I think the cost of board at a university is a fair approximation of the monthly cost of living off-campus with a roommate or roommates. Remember, however, off-campus apartments/houses tend to have 12-month leases, so your summer plans need to be considered.

<u>Working</u>

It's a myth that you can work your way through school. Wages, particularly for hourly jobs, have grown far, far slower than tuition (which grows almost 9% a year). It's also a myth that working will help you be more responsible, as it's demonstrably harmful to your GPA to work more than 15 hours a week.

Unless you're working at an internship or a job that will further your career, I think of working like taking student loans. It's necessary for many of you, but it's not an ideal outcome. Colleges are increasingly offering incentives in the form of grants and scholarships for students who agree to work no more than 10 – 20 hours a week. See if that's an option and consider borrowing more (if you can do so reasonably).

In This Section

Loans – If you have to borrow, borrow smart. Don't take it for granted that what Financial Aid offers you is the best deal.

Grants – There are more grants in the world than the Pell & the FSEOG. A lot of them go unclaimed.

Scholarships – The hunt for scholarship dollars doesn't have to end when you enroll. In fact, you can make a great return on your time by applying for scholarships throughout your college career.

Resources

Net Price Calculator	nces.ed.gov/collegenavigator/
EFC Calculator	finaid.org/calculators/finaidestimate.phtml
Financial Aid Guide	finaid.org
Average Cost of Attendance	collegescorecard.ed.gov

5 STUDENT LOANS

The Numbers

- 70% of students graduated with debt in 2016. The average debt for graduates was $37,172.
- 11.2% of borrowers are in default or 90+ days delinquent on their student loan payments.
- In 2016, about 36% of seniors planned to move back in with their parents after graduation.[1]

Good Debt, Bad Debt, Smart Debt, Dumb Debt

It's highly likely you'll go into debt, if not for undergrad then for graduate school. Not all debt is created equal. The cost of the debt (fees and interest) and the purpose of the debt (how you're really using it and what you'll get from it) are incredibly important.

Good debt is using all federal and state options (where state options exist) before darkening the door of a private student lender. Good debt is your last option. It's money borrowed after you've aggressively pursued grants and scholarships through your college, its foundation, and 3rd parties.

Bad debt is high interest private student loans (not all lenders offer the same terms), credit cards, or other short-term loans used to pay tuition and fees. The costs are exorbitant with substantial fees and high interest rates. Bear in mind, it'll probably be several years before you're actively paying down the debt you accrue, and a high interest rate will grow your debt massively.

---

[1] There are many valid reasons for moving back home, particularly saving money. It's become a popular option for millennials, because of lower wages, higher debt, and higher housing costs. I just don't want it to be the *only* option.

Smart debt is debt that leads to a career where you can pay off your debt while living independently and building your financial life. Smart debt is a tool, a means to an end. **Smart debt is borrowing at a level that is appropriate for your degree's earning potential and your field's job market.**

Dumb debt is money borrowed without a plan for how the money you borrow will turn into money earned. Dumb debt is borrowing to spend excessively, assuming you can pay the bill later. Dumb debt is borrowing money you don't need to, and/or borrowing money without considering all options on the table.

What Happens if Debt Goes Unchecked

If you read (and remember) the introduction to the book, I said the worst case scenario was for you to leave college with no degree and a mountain of debt. Now I am a few chapters older and wiser, but I stand by that claim. Leaving college without a degree and with a ton of debt is the worst outcome.

The second worst outcome is if debt hinders your ability to build a life. Uncontrolled debt can hurt your credit, your ability to save, your ability to live independently, and your ability to be financially secure as a young adult. Equally important, massive debt can force you to take jobs or pursue careers that you wouldn't otherwise. **Unchecked debt limits your options for years to come.**

Another lousy outcome is graduating in debt with few options to use your degree and low earnings potential. Some degrees earn more than others, that's a fact (check out the chapter on *Majors* for more). Some degrees have the potential to be lucrative, but for only a small percentage of recipients. It's perfectly fine to change your mind in adulthood and go back to school to change careers; it is not ideal, though, to have to go back to school because the degree you have is not marketable or the salaries you can command with that degree are insufficient for your needs or desired life.

For example, let's say you go to a small college in Appalachia. That college may have an excellent academic reputation, one that is well earned and have a rigorous graphic design program (your hypothetical major). Unfortunately, that college has little to no career services, and, because you're far from any significant sized city or major employer, your options for an internship are very limited. If you aren't willing to move from that area, and you aren't willing to go out and find your own internships, you may be wasting your money and time getting that particular degree.

If you're working in the public sector as a teacher, librarian, police officer, or government employee, you may qualify for significant loan forgiveness (check out the resources section at the end of the chapter). Remember, only federal loans can be forgiven.

How Students Get in Trouble & How to Avoid It

The loan amounts are abstract – Because you don't start paying right away, it's easy to lose track of exactly how much you're borrowing and what the payments will be. Large numbers become an abstraction. If I tell you, "one child was killed in a car accident," you'll probably feel more strongly than if I say, "1,000 people died in an earthquake." Why is that? Out of 1,000 people, there were assuredly many, many children, but the number 1,000 is so large that we can't really understand that scale on a personal level.

What to do: Every semester, evaluate what your loan payments will be in the future, for the current and previous semesters. There's a handy calculator listed in the resources section of this chapter. It can be scary to look at, I know, but it'll help you plan for your future and make you more mindful of your present expenses. There's nothing to be said for sticking your head in the sand.

Students are in a hurry to sign – It's easy to just sign your award letter semester after semester. While your financial aid office tries to max out your grants and low-cost loans, they may have missed something, or (equally likely) there are scholarships/grants that you qualify for but aren't currently receiving because they require an extra step on your part.

What to do: **Always bring your award letter to financial aid and discuss it.** See if you can get some grants or cheaper loan options. Talk to your department too, and see what they have to say. If you do this every semester, you will save yourself money. Talking to financial aid is particularly important if you or your family has experienced a significant financial change or hardship. I routinely hear of students who transferred schools to save money without ever talking to the financial aid department at their former institution.

They don't graduate on time – This is the number one cause of unmanageable student loan debt. Not only do you tack on semesters, or years, of debt, but you also run the risk of maxing out your lower cost federal loans.

What to do: This whole book is written with the express purpose of helping you graduate on time, so read it—after all, you own it. Common reasons for not graduating in four years are transferring colleges, changing majors later in college, poor academic performance, and not taking enough hours.

Government Loans vs. Private Loans

Government Loans

The Federal Government is the number one student lender in the country, and they run a slew of loan programs. Most students should exhaust all their federal options before considering private loans. All federal loans, except the Parent PLUS loan, have a lifetime max. If you transfer or take longer to graduate, you may run out of federal loans. **Only federal loans qualify for income-based repayment and forgiveness.**

Perkins – Perkins loans are a need-based loan that carry an interest rate of 5.5% and have a loan limit of $5,500 per year with a maximum of $27,500 in undergrad. Repayment doesn't start until nine months after you graduate, leave school, or drop below half-time status (6 hours per semester, or equivalent).

Your college is the lender, and not all colleges participate. When it comes time to pay, you'll probably make your payments to a loan servicer that has a contract with your college. Interest does not accrue (your balance stays the same) while you're in college. Qualifying for a Perkins loan does not mean you'll get one; they are distributed on a first come-first served basis. **File your FAFSA *early* every year!**

Subsidized Stafford Loans – Stafford loans are another subsidized, need-based loan. The rate on new loans varies, for 2018 it will be 4.45%. But once you borrow the money, the rate does not change. The yearly maximum for subsidized Stafford loans is $3,500 for freshmen, $4,500 for sophomores, and $5,500 for juniors and seniors. There is a maximum lifetime/total loan amount of $23,000. The yearly and lifetime maximums are the same for financially independent and dependent students. After you graduate, leave school, or drop below half-time, you have a six month grace period to begin your payments.

Unsubsidized Stafford Loans – Unsubsidized loans carry the same interest rates, but interest accrues while you're still attending college. The maximum loan amount per year and lifetime maximum changes depending on your financial status. Financially dependent students are limited to $2,000 a year and a cap of subsidized + unsubsidized = $31,000. Independent students can borrow $6,500 a year as freshmen and sophomores and $7,500 as juniors and seniors for a lifetime maximum of subsidized + unsubsidized = $57,500. After you graduate, leave school, or drop below half-time, you have a six month grace period to begin your payments.

Parent PLUS – You cosign a loan with your parent. To receive a Parent PLUS loan, your parents will have to pass a credit check, but the credit check has a low bar and most pass. Parent PLUS loans have very large loan maximums; you can borrow the entire cost of attendance minus any financial aid you have received: grants, scholarships, and direct loans. <u>Parent PLUS loans accrue interest and have payments due immediately.</u> The loan length is ten years. The interest rate is fixed at 7.0%. Be careful with these loans, and be mindful of what you can afford right now. In some cases, PLUS loans may end up being more expensive than private loans or other options (a home equity loan, for example).

HRSA Loans – Health Resource & Service Administration loans are available for students in a health professional program: medical (M.D./D.O.) school, nursing school, occupational therapy school, physical therapy school, optometry, pharmacy, dentistry, and others qualify. HRSA loans are need-based and competitive, but the loans themselves are worth it because much of the debt can be discharged after graduation.

There are several loan programs for different professions, but the loan limits are fairly high, up to tuition plus cost of living (even more for 3rd and 4th year medical students). Interest rates are capped at 5%. There is a grace period of one year after graduation or leaving the program, during which there are no payments and interest does not accrue. The loan period is 10 years.

Paying Back Government Loans

Depending on your career and employer, you may not have to pay back all of your loans. If your income is low, you can make income-based repayments.

Seek Forgiveness – Various government programs allow forgiveness for a portion or all of your loans if you work in specified fields at qualifying institutions. For example, teachers can have $17,500 or their entire Perkins loan balance forgiven if they teach at a qualifying school (typically in an underserved, underperforming district) for five years.

The Public Service Loan Forgiveness program will forgive the balance of your direct loans after you make ten years (120 total) payments. You have to work for the government or a 501(c)(3) non-profit. Peace Corps volunteers, medical professionals working with the indigent or in underserved areas, and others can receive loan forgiveness.

If, however, you're a contractor for a company working for the federal government (increasingly common), you will not receive loan forgiveness. In the resources, you'll find a link to saltmoney.org. Saltmoney has a free eBook with details on over 100 forgiveness programs (check the resources section of this chapter).

Income-Based Repayment – Income-based repayment programs allow federal loan payments to be more manageable. There are four income based repayment plans, three (IBR, PAYE, REPAYE) set a bottom payment level as 10% to 15% of your discretionary income and a maximum payment level as the 10-year standard repayment amount. Repayment under the first three plans lasts 20 years. The fourth plan (ICR) stipulates you pay either 20% of your discretionary income or what you would pay on a repayment plan over 12 years, adjusted to your income. Repayment under ICR takes 25 years.

Forgiveness and income-based repayment is the <u>only</u> way to get out from under your student loans. Student loans are almost never discharged or forgiven, even in bankruptcy. The only other options for discharging your student loan debt aren't really options at all: death, total and permanent disability, or your college closing while you're still earning your degree.

Private Student Loans

Only consider private student loans after you have tapped out your grants, scholarships, and federal student loans. Always compare any private loan options against the Parent Plus Loans; Parent PLUS loans are often cheaper. **Private student loans are more expensive than government options, and private loans are not eligible for income based repayment or forgiveness.**

The Technical Stuff – The best student loans have an interest rate of LIBOR plus ~2.0% or PRIME minus 0.5%.

Cosigner – Rates that are competitive with PLUS loans are usually only available for students who have cosigners with very good credit. Not having a cosigner or having a cosigner with poor credit will steeply impact your rates and the amount of money you can borrow. Less than 10% of undergrads can qualify for a private student loan without a cosigner.

Don't Just Shop Rates – Lower rate loans often hide fees. To better compare, consider that 3 to 4% in fees is roughly equivalent to 1% of additional interest. **Beware of rates that are low while you're in college but jump as soon as you graduate or leave school.**

Fixed vs. Variable Rates – Fixed rates stay the same regardless of what happens to interest rates at large. Variable rates will change as interest rates go up and down. Variable rates often start cheaper but can end up being significantly more expensive if rates go up considerably. Watch out for hidden fees in both loan types.

Applying Without a Cosigner

You need a credit history for a private student loan, and you can't get one overnight. If you've been in the military or are a nontraditional student, it's likely you've acquired some credit history. If you're coming straight from high school, you are unlikely to have significant credit history.

Building credit is all about having bills and paying them on time. Check out the *Checklist: Your Credit* for how to do this.

Bad Credit/No Cosigner

You'll need a credit score between 600 and 700 to qualify for a private student loan. Don't assume your credit is bad; obtain a free credit score. I like creditkarma.com for monitoring my credit.

Do everything you can to avoid paying tuition with credit cards or high-interest personal loans.

Resources

Loan Payment Calculator	finaid.org/calculators/loanpayments.phtml
Assorted Loan Calculators	lendedu.com/blog/student-loan-calculators
Forgiveness Programs	saltmoney.org/content/media/eBook/100-ways-to-get-rid-of-student-loans-without-paying-them/_/R-101-22831

6 GRANTS

Grants are free money. You don't have to repay them, and you don't (usually) have to write essays for them. What you may not know, is that aside from federal grants, there are hundreds of ways to get state, local, foundation, and private grants.

Federal Grants

Federal grants are need-based, so filing your FAFSA—and filing it early—is vital. While grants are free money, you may have to pay them back if you drop in status from full-time to part-time, drop below part-time, or you withdraw from college.

Pell Grants – Pell grants are the largest grant. Pell grants are given in varying amounts depending on need-based. There are four criteria for Pell grants: financial need beyond Expected Family Contribution, at least 6 hours (or equivalent) enrollment, cost of attendance, and yearlong enrollment (fall & spring) as a student. The maximum per year is $5,500 but can vary due to how much funding is available for Pell Grants. The lifetime max is 6 years of funding (the current max would be $5,500 x 6 = $33,000).

FSEOG – The Federal Supplemental Educational Opportunity Grant is a campus-based grant program that helps students in difficult financial positions. There is limited funding for this grant, so students with an Expected Family Contribution of zero are considered first. **Do your FAFSA as early as possible for your best shot at this grant.** FSEOG grants go up to $4,000 per year, but most students receive much less.

TEACH Grants – TEACH grants are available for students who agree to teach four years in a public school or educational services agency that serves low-income families. Not all colleges/universities participate in the TEACH grant program. If you receive a TEACH grant but do not fulfill the teaching requirement, your grant converts to an unsubsidized student loan.

Iraq & Afghanistan Service Grants – Your eligible for this grant if your parent or guardian died during military service in Iraq or Afghanistan.

Foster Care – If you were adopted out of foster care or were in foster care after the age of 13, you are automatically an independent student on your FAFSA. There's no specific grant, but you'll get the maximum grant amounts and the best deal on loan dollars.

State Grants

Many states offer grants based on need, minority status, major, and/or merit. Google "Your State and college grants" and you should find some helpful information. Remember, this is the government, so web design and organization can be a bit haphazard and you may find multiple pages with different grants. In the resources section of this chapter, I've included a link that has grants sorted by state (it is generally up-to-date, but I would look independently).

Institutional Grants

Colleges and universities are the second largest grant provider. These grants can be based on need, minority status, major, career goal, and/or merit. Institutional grants can be scattered all over the place. Ask your financial aid counselor, but also ask your department, appropriate professional societies, minority organizations, and religious organizations.

Colleges and universities often have an emergency fund available to students in dire circumstances. Don't be afraid to ask, to ask more than once, or to ask more than one department. Be aggressive.

Foundation & Organization Grants

You can find grant funding from corporate and individual foundations and non-profits. These grants are usually for specific populations or for specific majors. If you're the first in your family to attend college, Sallie Mae (the student loan people), among others, fund grants. These grants are competitive, so put the work in on the application.

If you're a single parent, a minority, a nontraditional student, come from a military family, have a disability, have a chronic health condition, have experienced a tragic loss there may be a grant for you. If you've got a particular field in mind, are passionate about a particular cause or policy, have a hobby or interest that defines you, a religious affiliation, a parent employed by a major corporation, a parent who works for a nonprofit, a parent who is a small business person, there may be a grant for you. Get the idea? It's likely you can find a grant or grants that fit you.

Getting Grants

1. **File Your FAFSA** – You need to fill out an updated FAFSA every year. For more on the FAFSA, check out the chapter at the beginning of this section.

2. **File your FAFSA ASAP** – Many grants are first come, first serve at the state and federal level. The sooner you file your FAFSA, the better off you are. (It's important enough that I listed it twice).

3. **Determine if you need to file a CSS Profile** – Many private colleges and foundations use the CSS either in conjunction or in lieu of the FAFSA.

4. **See What's Available** – Here are places to start your search: financial aid office, departmental office, applicable organizations.

5. **Use FastWeb or Scholarships.com** – Complete out, or update, a profile to see what you could be eligible for on either or both of those websites. These are good aggregators, but they are by no means comprehensive, and should be used to augment your search, not define it.

6. **Don't Give Up** – Check back every semester and every year to see if you can get more free money. It's a little time for a potentially huge payoff.

Resources

Federal Grants	studentaid.ed.gov/sa/types/grants-scholarships
State Grants	nasfaa.org/State_Financial_Aid_Programs
Grant Watch	grantwatch.com/cat/15/higher-education-grants.html

7 SCHOLARSHIPS

Colleges and universities are, by far, the biggest dispenser of college dollars. For most of you, the bulk of your scholarship dollars will come from your future alma mater.

But don't forget about external scholarships. Every year, I push students to apply for as many scholarships as possible, and, unfortunately, I am always disappointed by their lack of enthusiasm. You'd be surprised at how a little effort and the willingness to take the chance can pay off big.

My brother spent two hours writing an essay for a small foundation. That essay earned him $500 per year for four years of undergraduate *and* $500 for each year of his doctorate. He earned a total of $4,500 for about two hours of work, or 2,250 dollars per hour.

"Sure," you say, "that worked for him, but he got lucky." That's a reasonable argument, so let's say he wasn't as successful with his applications. Let's say he applied for ten scholarships identical to the one above, but he only won one out of the ten. In that hypothetical, my poor brother would have earned a measly $225 an hour.

Don't Stop Applying

While it's true that the majority of scholarship dollars are earmarked for incoming freshmen, the hunt for scholarships does not end on the first day of class your freshmen year. In fact, you should be applying for scholarships *throughout college*.

For sophomores and upperclassmen, your school offers scholarship opportunities, particularly within your department. Once you pick a field/career, look for scholarships from professional societies and industry.

You'll also find scholarship opportunities in student organizations, from honors societies to fraternities/sororities. The money is there, but you have to look a little harder. The good news is that these scholarships are less competitive, as students are even more apathetic about hunting scholarships once they're in college.

Speak to your financial aid counselor every time you go in to sign your financial aid paperwork. Ask the department chair of your major. And keep up on fastweb.com and scholarships.com.

Institutional Scholarships

When you apply as a freshman or as a transfer student, you'll automatically be considered for (some, not all) academic scholarships upon your application. Apply for college as early as possible, it helps your admissions chances, and most scholarships are first come, first served.

Automatic Awards – The most common academic scholarships are given at breakpoints in SAT/ACT score & GPA. For example, a middle tier scholarship may require a 27 on the ACT (or SAT equivalent) and 3.5 GPA.

Automatic + Essay – Higher tier scholarships typically have a higher breakpoint, for example, a 30 or 32 on the ACT and a 3.8+ GPA. Once you hit the breakpoint, a committee will take a look at one or more of your admissions essays to make a set number of awards.

Separate Application – The most elite awards usually require a separate application. Students have to have earned the highest automatic tier award and are then invited to apply for these prestigious scholarships. Students often do a mediocre job on these applications, particularly if they're for a safety school. Don't. Aside from being very lucrative, these top awards often offer special opportunities. This level of award can make a safety school more competitive *and* you may not get into any other school. I made this mistake myself.

Departmental – Departments within colleges often offer scholarships or grants for research, study abroad, conference attendance, and general purpose. These scholarships usually require a second application, which varies from simple to involved. Take advantage of these opportunities, surprisingly few students apply, and they are not as competitive as you may think.

Special Populations – Colleges and Universities often have individually vested scholarships designated for members of a religious, ethnic, or racial group. You may be considered for these automatically if you have checked off any demographic information on your application. Don't rely on that though; investigate potential sources of funding by speaking to your financial aid counselor.

Other Scholarships

Create an account at fastweb.com and scholarships.com. Fill out a profile and you'll be matched to appropriate scholarship offerings. The search doesn't end there, make sure you think about other likely sources like your parent's employer, local religious organizations/national religious organizations, local foundations, and the local chamber of commerce. <u>A rule of thumb is that the harder the scholarship is to find, the easier it is to get.</u>

Professional Societies/Careers – Professional societies often offer scholarships with applications and awards that vary quite a bit. Often, these come with no-strings-attached, meaning you can change goals without having to pay back the money. Women who have a STEM major are doubly encouraged to look into this. Fastweb.com and Scholarships.com is a great source for finding these, but you can also speak to your financial aid counselor and any organizations active on campus.

Foundations & Corporations – Most large corporations have a foundation attached to them, as do extremely wealthy individuals. Typically, these foundations offer scholarships. You'll find that the amount varies from a few hundred to several thousand dollars which are given either as a lump sum or on a yearly basis. These scholarships may require an essay, minimum GPA, and test score. The effort is worth it, though, as there are far fewer applications than you'd think. In fact, over 1.9 billion dollars goes unclaimed due to lack of qualified applicants.

Resources

Scholarship Matching Services	Fastweb.com
	Scholarships.com
	bigfuture.collegeboard.org/scholarship-search

8 BUILDING A HAPPY LIFE
Happiness, A Good Life, Homesickness, & Social Media

I was skeptical of the importance of happiness for much of my life. I had the view that happiness was not an objective in-and-of itself. Being happy, I thought, was supposed to be the incidental consequence of making all the right decisions. To those of you who think that happiness is bullshit, unobtainable, or irrelevant I'd encourage you to think of happiness as a goal—maybe the most important goal. Even reaching for happiness will make you happier. Remember, happiness isn't a uniform state—you'll always have bad days, like bad weather, but shoot for an emotional climate of overall happiness.

If you're having trouble seeing anything positive in your life, or stress level is unmanageable, consider seeing a counselor. I do it, and I have for years. There's no shame in it; it's confidential and really helps. Check out the *Mental Health* chapter for more.

Happy people have higher GPA's. It's easy to fall into the trap of thinking that success requires suffering—we've all seen movies where characters fall asleep over open textbooks. This is real life, and you aren't a machine, and, as much as you try, you can't live like one.

We tend to think of happiness as the enemy of success, but it's the opposite. **Lasting success requires happiness.** Work is work, and it can be uncomfortable. But working shouldn't be consistently painful. If it is, evaluate what you're doing, how you're doing it, and how you're living the rest of your life.

Having friends and being involved are predictors of success. Students who are involved and have a good social support network do better in college, are more likely to finish college, and are more likely to get admitted to a graduate program or get a job that aligns with their career goals.

Defining Happiness & A Good Life

How you define happiness is up to you, but you should have a definition. If you start making choices with the goal of maximizing your long-term (not the quick payoff) happiness, you will end up happier.

If you don't define what you want out of life, you'll bump your way through until, one day, you realize that you're letting your life be defined for you. If you don't spend time thinking and planning, you'll always be reacting to the circumstances you're dealt.

I can't tell you what *your* good life looks like; it's different for everyone. It is a reflection of your values, your choices, and your experiences. What I can say is that a good life isn't just good grades, financial success, or a fancy title. A good life is one that fits you, and if you define that for yourself, you'll go after that life—even unconsciously. (Please check out the chapter on *Goal Setting*).

For me, a good life involves helping my students and my readers, being a good dad, staying physically active, choosing projects and work intentionally, and being able to support my family and save enough money to send my daughter to college and me to the old folk's home. You can also say I *need* those things. I work to foster and protect my needs, and they provide the foundation of what I consider a good life.

I *need* my daughter, and, like most parents, would sacrifice my life for her. Hopefully it never comes to that, but parenting itself is an act of happy sacrifice. My *need* for my daughter makes any cost worth paying.

Aside from my daughter, the freedom and flexibility of self-employment are the most important to me. I don't care to be rich, though I'll take donations, but I *need* freedom over how I spend my time and which projects and students I take on.

I *need* that flexibility to be happy (or at least I'm pretty sure I do). Certainly, I could live by working an office job, and I did so for many years. I worked towards a point where I could work for myself, and largely from home. It's made a huge difference in the quality of my life, and it's all because I recognized that I *needed* that flexibility.

You may not know your needs now, and those needs may change, but start thinking about them. Most of all, start prioritizing what's important to you: life is a series of tradeoffs, and you need to be aware of what bargains you want to make.

Choose Your Circle Carefully

I urge you to associate and be friendly with a wide array of people— particularly those you disagree with. But choose those closest to you carefully (including what organizations you're heavily involved in).

You'll certainly affect those around you, but their effects on you will be greater than you realize. Choose people who value you, respect you, and will help you. **Choose people you want to be like because you will become more like them**. Jim Rohn wrote that "You are the average of the five people you spend the most time with." I think there's quite a bit of truth to that.

Not Risky Risk Taking

So many social interactions seem incredibly risky. Saying "hello" to someone is not risky (even though you feel like it is), nor is trying out a student organization. At worst, you get snubbed by the jerk you said hello to, or you waste an hour of your time at a meeting. While being slighted or feeling out of place is uncomfortable, even painful, neither is actually harming you.

I'm not encouraging the reckless use of alcohol or other substances, nor am I suggesting you put yourself in unsafe situations. But, responsible social risks aren't risks at all, once you consider that no real harm can befall you. What I am suggesting is that you learn to be at ease with being in new social situations. The only way to do that is to get out there and try (check out the *Meeting People* and *Getting Involved Chapters*).

As someone who is (probably) somewhat older than you, I would say that regretting missed opportunities lasts far longer than the discomfort of taking a shot and coming up short.

Start Early

Start building your new life as soon as you've unloaded the car and started settling in. You don't know what shape that new life is going to take, so start by casting a wide net. Meet as many people as you can, begin to develop relationships, and get involved on campus. Start deciding who you want to be, because if you don't pick, you'll become someone anyway.

...But It's Never Too Late

That said, it's never too late to start defining yourself. Try out some new hobbies, join some student organizations, and hang out with different groups of people. Learn to say no, just because you've done something in the past, doesn't mean you have to continue down the same path.

It Takes Time

You won't build your life in the first week, or first month, or first semester, or maybe even your first year. It takes time to get your footing, explore the options, and establish a routine. It takes time to build meaningful friendships. You start one day at a time, and a lot of things you try won't end up amounting to much.

Try and keep trying. That's all you have to do.

Homesickness

Homesickness affects ~70% of college freshmen. It's a normal response, and the only thing wrong with being homesick is that it sucks. Homesickness can occur at any time, from move-in day to months later as the work piles up and the novelty of college dies back. It often strikes when you get sick or during busy periods, like midterms and finals. Homesickness can, however, occur in conjunction with other problems (check out the *Mental Health* chapter).

College puts you outside your comfort zone. You knew how things work at home, but now the rules, the people, and the expectations are very different. You don't feel as secure because you're not sure what to expect. **To defeat homesickness, you have to psychologically create a new home at college.** (after all, you can't be homesick at college if you think of college as your home). **In fact, you can use homesickness as an advantage. Use the discomfort you feel currently as motivation to build a great life right away.** Here are some steps you can follow:

1. Start making friends and get involved on campus (check out *Meeting People* and *Getting Involved* for more). If you're very homesick, then I strongly recommend you get involved on campus right away. If you're busy, you won't have the time or the inclination to be homesick.

2. Establish some "spots" for yourself. Maybe it's a table at the library, a corner of the student union, or a coffee shop.

3. Talk to family and friends from home, but not too much.

4. Seek help from other students or a counselor if you're having a tough time.

5. Remember that you aren't alone, about 7 out of 10 college freshmen are homesick at some point.

Homesickness is fixable, but you are the only one who can treat it. Eventually, the goal is to feel homesick when *you leave college* because you've transferred your "home allegiance" to school.

Please don't consider transferring schools right away. Please don't drop out. If you are thinking of transferring because you feel homesick or you feel your school is a bad fit, **give the school one full year**. Stay positive, a year is a wonderful length of time. **It's short enough that it's only a small percentage of your life, but it's just long enough that anything can happen.**

Social Media & Connectivity

I really wanted to go with a "cutting the cord" play on words here. I tried "cutting the wireless" but thought it was confusing and you'd probably miss the joke. It also wasn't especially funny.

That aside, it's easier to stay homesick than ever before. You already know what I'm talking about: social media, facetime, text messages, and so on. You also already know or have an idea of how much time you spend on Snapchat, Facebook, Instagram, etc.

A virtual life is no replacement for a real life. Far-flung friends from high school can't split a pizza with your or let you borrow their lecture notes.

But aside from the practical aspects of friendship, there is a quality and depth to in-person interactions that is lacking in online only relationships.

Staying in touch with family and high school friends is important and, in fact, can keep you from feeling homesick and make you feel more attached to your college. Like anything though, the key is moderation, and—of course—what works for you will be a personal decision.

Here's are some questions to ask yourself about your social media use. Use these to evaluate your connectivity and decide whether you need to move things more to the "in-person" side of the balance.

- Who do I call/text/chat/facetime/skype with most? What am I using those interactions for?

- Do I spend more time interacting with people in-person, or through devices?

- Do I turn down real-life social invitations to spend time on social media or talking to friends/family from home?

- Do I "hide behind" my phone whenever I'm faced with a new social situation?

- Am I, if I'm honest with myself, do I use technology because I'm afraid of meeting people?

In general, social media and connectivity enhance the student experience. But, be mindful of what you do on social media and **why** you're using it.

One More Thing About Social Media…

I think social media can be a powerful tool for connecting with your college, staying in touch with people, and forming new relationships. For most students, social media is beneficial. But, I'm going to join the countless others who have warned you about the pitfalls of social media. If someone is harassing you or bullying you, block them and/or report them to the college and police.

Don't send naked pictures/videos to others. I don't care how much you love them. If someone has naked pictures/videos and tries to use them against you, or disseminate them, that's a criminal act in many states

(Revenge Porn Laws). Also, don't be an idiot and post hate speech, drunken photos, or the like. Be careful meeting strangers from Tinder and the like, and always make sure someone knows where you are and who you are with.

I also want to talk to you about how I use social media. I don't put pictures of myself up where it looks like I have a double chin or a gut. I only post pictures of my daughter when I feel like "people will think this is so cute and that my kid is the best of all possible kids." And I only post about work or my personal life when something exciting happens.

Do you see a pattern? **I'm narcissistic about what I put on social media.** I always want to have the best family, be good looking (insomuch as possible), and have the most fascinating career and life. This is how people use social media, but we forget that everyone is doing the same thing.

Everyone posts the *best possible things about themselves,* even to the point of exaggerating into falsehood. When you compare or compete with your friends on social media, you're not giving yourself a fair shake. They live regular lives too, they eat, they sleep, they poop, and they have bad days.

Long Distance Relationships

I'm fighting the temptation to explain why you should break up with boyfriend/girlfriend who goes to a different college or is still in high school. I won't though, and occasionally these relationships prosper and both parties are happy and grow together. Statistics on the duration of these relationships isn't readily available, but, in my experience, the likelihood of a "happily ever after" seems small.

It's easy to idealize a boyfriend/girlfriend who is absent. In fact, many students break up soon after reuniting in person. You become reacquainted with their flaws in person and may feel let down because you've idealized them to the point that they can no longer meet your expectations. Additionally, you've both changed, and those changes may have taken you in different directions.

You can't ever talk anyone out of a relationship (it's a great way to lose a friend), so I'm not going to try. And, in fairness, it may work out wonderfully for you. But please remember that you need a life outside of your romantic partner. Establish that life, and if your partner has a problem with your independence and ability to be happy while away from them, you should end the relationship.

In This Section

Meeting People – A good social support system is critical to your success in college. It's also a necessary component of being happy (which in itself is critical to your success). I go over how to meet people at different stages of your college career.

Getting Involved – Students who are involved on campus have higher GPAs and more opportunities. Aside from the interpersonal and leadership skills you can acquire, you'll meet likeminded people and have more opportunities available to you.

Roommates – Your roommate is your first taste of married life (in some ways, at least). The relationship is equally important as it can make you miserable or can improve the quality of your life. Problems with roommates are the most frequent cause of students transferring schools and a highly ranked cause of students dropping out.

Living in a Dorm – Where you live affects who you meet and what your peer group is like. Evaluate your options carefully to decide what's best for you.

Resources

Social Media Use Disorder	psychologytoday.com/us/blog/your-online-secrets/201710/do-you-have-social-media-disorder
Long Distance Relationships & College	overcomingthedistance.com/advice/long-distance-relationships-in-college/

9 MEET PEOPLE

Meeting people is critical to feeling at home at college. Not only does it make life better, but you need a support system to succeed. For some of you, meeting people may be more difficult than the toughest class you'll ever take.

You Just Moved In

For the most part, freshmen who go away to school either know very few people—holdovers from high school—or they only know a few people that they want to associate with.

It's a very surreal moment; you're in an entirely new environment, and you're on your own for the first time. Not only that, but you don't know many people (at least people you want to know).

Here's the secret: **everyone feels the same way you do.**

The *idea* of meeting people may be terrifying, but *actually meeting* people is really easy. Follow these steps:

1. **Smile** – Smiling is great. If you're not a smiler, don't worry. There are a ton of other ways to exude friendliness. Make eye contact and give a friendly nod or gesture. Making eye contact (no crazy-murder eyes, please) is a great way to indicate to someone that you've noticed them and you're interested in talking.

2. **Say Hello** – Say hi to everyone you walk by in the hallway of your dorm. It doesn't have to turn into a conversation, and you shouldn't feel like it needs to. It does establish you as a friendly person.

3. **Offer to Help** – If you're all settled in, offer to lend someone a hand. It's a great way to meet people.

4. **Be Genuine** – Don't ever force yourself to feel or act a certain way. When you meet people and talk to them, be who you are. Talk about your background and your interests and look for common ground. Ultimately, you want to connect with people who like and respect you, so don't be afraid to be yourself (or say, "I don't know").

5. **Ask People About Themselves** – Show an interest in other people, if they say they played soccer in high school, ask them what they played. It's ok if you don't know what a midfielder is, you can ask that next. People respond positively if you show an interest in them.

6. **Remember Them** – Try and remember names and personal details. I'm terrible at names, but I learned a helpful trick: repeat their name three times in the course of the conversation, just don't do it all right together. For example, "Hey Dan, nice to meet you," then, sometime later, "That's cool Dan, what did you play in band?" And finally, "Good meeting you Dan, I'll catch you later."

7. **Get to Know Your Floor & Your Dorm** – Get to know your neighbors. You don't have to be friends with them, but it's nice to be on good terms with everyone (whenever possible). That said, don't feel like you always have to leave your door open or say "yes" to requests. One of the challenges of living in a dorm is having a semblance of personal space. You'll have to use trial and error to decide your own balance.

8. **Go to Events** – The first weekend of college feels a bit like a field trip. You'll be rounded up by your RA and marched (not literally, unless it *is* literally) to freshmen convocation, ice cream socials, etc. I won't lie, they can be kind of lame—just like those icebreakers you had to do at your floor meeting—but a lot of the "lame" feeling comes from the event's inherent awkwardness. Everyone feels a little like they're at a middle-school dance, so be the person that's totally OK with it, laughs along, and has a good time.

9. **Sit with People at Meals** – If you see a person, or a few people at a table, say hello and ask if you can join them. If it's easier for you, sit diagonally from them, so nobody feels pressure to engage. That way, you can start a conversation at your own pace.

10. **Invite People to Meals** – Ask your roommate, or someone down the hall, or someone from your last class if they want to grab a bite.

11. **Student Organizations** – I cover this in more detail in the "Getting Involved" chapter, but, seriously, **get involved**. Go to meetings and/or join a team for an organization/intramural league that you're interested in. There, you'll automatically find some people who share a common interest. Also, don't be afraid to get dragged to a meeting you don't think you'll like. You may be surprised, and, even if you aren't, you'll still meet some people (and maybe get free food).

Living At Home/Living Off-Campus

If you're living at home, you're likely attending a college with a fair number of students from your high school. I suggest you expand your circle by hanging out with people you went to high school with but didn't spend time with.

Watch out for groups from your high school who exclusively hang out with people from your town or high school, it can feel comfortable, but associating with them exclusively is likely going to stunt your social circle.

If you're away from home and living in an apartment, it can be a little trickier. I strongly suggest you live in a dorm freshman year (at least), but if you were initially waitlisted, changed your plans, or were the victim of some unfortunate institutional screw-up, that may not be possible.

Here are a few steps you can take to broaden your social network and build your support system whether you are living at home or off-campus:

Get Involved – If you aren't in a dorm, it's even more crucial that you get involved on campus. Check out the *Getting Involved* chapter for more.

Go to the Gym/Take a Fitness Class – Your student fitness center is a good place to meet a friend or two. You may end up in a spontaneous conversation with someone, or, if you keep a regular schedule, you'll start to recognize people with similar schedules, and, sooner or later, a conversation will strike up. Word to the polite, though, don't interrupt people when you're working out.

Attend Events – Go ahead and go to some of the events your school sponsors. It won't kill you, and you'll find people like you. Definitely make the effort to go to football games and popular sporting events—even if you're not a fan.

Later On

It's not too late. Maybe some of your friends transferred, or you've grown apart. Maybe you realize that you need a change. You're not beholden to anyone. Start meeting people, go to different organizations and events, follow the steps above.

10 GET INVOLVED

Why it Matters

It's good for your resume. Employers and graduate schools like to see that you're well rounded and capable of doing more than just getting A's.

It's good for your grades. Students who are involved have higher GPA's, higher graduation rates, and better time management skills. (You can, however, be over-involved and suffer a GPA drop).

You meet new people. Some will be OK, some will suck, and a few will be friends for the rest of your life.

It's good for your wellbeing. Aside from meeting new friends who share a common interest, pursuit, cause, or identity, you'll also find that you feel more of a bond with your college and a clearer sense of identity.

You get opportunities. Scholarships, internships, research opportunities, competitions, mentorship, and jobs after graduation all can be found through membership in student organizations.

You develop skills. You'll learn quite a bit about teamwork and leadership—should you take a leadership role, and you should. You may also learn something about budgeting and, depending on the organization, how to work with large unruly bureaucracies, i.e., your college.

You discover things about yourself. Finding things you love also means finding things you hate. Knowing what you like and what you don't like are critical to having a happy, self-determined life. Always try something once, even if you're pretty sure you'll hate it.

What to Look For in an Organization

People you want to be like – Pick organizations where you can look up to some members as models of how you want your career as a student to go. (I don't mean for you to emulate them in every way). The more time you plan on spending with that organization (this is particularly true of fraternities and sororities) the more important this is.

People you like – I don't mean for you to find a group of people that are identical to you; I mean people that you feel comfortable with or can grow to feel comfortable with.

Something you're passionate about – The more passion you have for the organization's purpose (even if it is wholly recreational), the more you'll get out of belonging.

How to Get Involved

Getting involved on campus is super easy, but, like meeting people, it can feel incredibly difficult. **To get involved on campus, you have to do three things: sign up, show up, and speak up.**

If someone from your floor asks you to a meeting, go ahead and go, even if you don't think you'll like it. Worst case scenario you waste an hour of your time (although you're likely to get pizza if it's towards the beginning of the year). In the beginning of the section, I talk about choosing your circle carefully, because who you spend time with helps define who you are. **Use student organizations to explore who you want to be.**

Orientation – Representatives from a wide array of student organizations will either present or have booths. Stop by anything that looks interesting. Sign-up on their email list (even if you aren't sure), and they'll let you know what their organization is up to once the semester starts.

On Campus – The first few weeks of the semester will be full of booths and tables in the student union, flyers on billboards and being handed out, and people with clipboards. Try some things out, see what you like. There's no obligation to go back, and no one will be hurt or mad if you don't.

Student Organizations Office – Your school will have an office dedicated to dealing with student organizations. They'll have a directory of organizations as well as contact information and meeting schedules. The Student Organization Office is also where you'd go if you wanted to start a student organization.

Fraternities & Sororities – Social fraternities and sororities have rush periods, structured activities after which the pledging cycle begins. Social fraternities and sororities are discussed in more detail later in this chapter.

Service Organizations & Fraternities – You'll find booths/tables for service organizations and fraternities at the beginning of the school year. Service fraternities have a pledging period (like social fraternities/sororities), and pledging is very time-consuming.

Intramurals – Signups for intramurals are held during the first few weeks of the semester. At some colleges, you may need to go to an office to register. You'll either signup as a team (which means recruiting a team) or asked to be assigned to a team. If you want to play, don't hesitate to sign up alone. There's a good chance you'll make some friends on your new team. There are also leagues and tournaments throughout the semester if you don't sign up initially.

Student Government – Your school's student government will have regular meetings and you should be able to find the schedule easily. Just show up. People in student government want you involved, there's always a committee or a project to volunteer for. Go to a meeting and if you see something that you're interested in, speak up.

Campus Media – Your school has a newspaper, magazine, literary journal, radio station, television station, or all of the above. Depending on what you want your involvement to be, you may have to apply or audition. Be patient; you aren't going to be the opinion editor of the newspaper your first day on the job. Be OK starting with more grunt work and less glamour.

Honors Societies – You have to be invited to join an honor society. Be careful with honor societies. There are a lot of "fake" honor societies that will take your money and confer no benefit to you. If your invitation comes to your parent's address and the organization is not active on your campus, it's probably a scam. Do some research, if your invitation is from a for-profit company, that's a huge red flag (note: a .org web address does not mean that the organization is non-profit).

Types of Organizations

Major/Academic Organizations – These are, perhaps, the most common student organization. You'll find various societies on many college campuses. Don't neglect these; they can provide scholarship opportunities, as well as career-specific experience that looks great on your resume. You'll also benefit from having access to students in your major who may have some insight as to what professors to take/avoid and how to navigate the department.

Religious/Spiritual Organizations – You'll find dozens of religious organizations on college campuses representing most major religions. These can be great resources for students of faith, or who are curious about faith. On most campuses you'll find an organization that fits your level of religious involvement (there are organizations that fit even the most casual of church goers).

Diversity/Cultural – There are a ton of student organizations for students with different ethnicities, sexual orientations, and cultures. These are invaluable for international students, LGBTQ students, and students who closely identify with their culture. They provide support, community, advocacy, and the opportunity to educate others. I strongly recommend checking out these organizations if you belong to a community which helps define you.

Political/Cause Organizations – You'll find organizations for political parties as well as platforms. Often, campus party organizations (college democrats, college republicans, etc.) are active in local campaigns. If you are interested in politics, these are invaluable organizations.

If you don't like politics much, but love—for example—the environment, then check out organizations like the Sierra Club. These clubs not only do community service and outreach, but they often pair with the college/university to achieve larger initiatives.

Recreational/Leisure – I think all organizations should be fun, and if you hate going then don't. But some organizations are meant solely for fun. Outdoor activity clubs, music groups, DJ clubs, film clubs, etc. If you've got an interest, check them out, even if you haven't done the activity before.

Service Organizations – Most student organizations participate in some community service, particularly around the holidays. Some organizations, however, are made specifically for service. You'll find general volunteer organizations and organizations with a special purpose. Either is great, but special purpose organizations like Engineers Without Borders and the Food Recovery Network can be huge resume boosters and help you acquire career-related skills.

Service Fraternities – Service fraternities are co-educational groups that offer a close-knit community like a social fraternity or sorority but with an organizational focus on community service. There are several service fraternities, Alpha Phi Omega and Epsilon Sigma Alpha are two notable examples. Unlike a traditional student organization, there is a pledge period, Greek rituals, and such. Like social fraternities/sororities, service fraternities are a serious time commitment. Many students center their campus lives around service fraternity involvement.

Service Fraternities are great organizations and I strongly recommend them, particularly for people who are having a hard time finding "their tribe." Be cautious though, like any organization that takes quite a bit of time, you can become overly committed to a service fraternity, which could negatively impact your grades.

Social Fraternities & Sororities – Social fraternities and sororities differ widely from campus to campus. Joining a fraternity or sorority is a substantial time commitment both during the pledging process and when you're an active member.

To join a fraternity/sorority you have to go through a process called "rush". *Informal rushes* are where students show up to the fraternity/sorority house or a meeting place and meet the active chapter. These are casual events and there's usually food served (no alcohol though). *Formal rush* is run by the university and Greek organization governing bodies. You'll have to sign up in order to be eligible to join a fraternity.

Many colleges or universities prohibit freshmen rushing in their first semester or first year. I think waiting to rush is a good idea. Pledging is incredibly time intensive, and you need to get your feet under you socially and academically before you take on a fraternity/sorority.

Once you express interest in a fraternity/sorority, you'll receive a bid *if the fraternity/sorority wants you to join.* This can be done very informally, or very formally through a ranking system. Once you formally accept the bid, you've begun the pledging process.

Should I join? I don't know. I don't know you, and it's likely I don't know your college's Greek community. At some schools, Greek life is incredibly popular and up to 40% of students participate. At other schools, Greek life comprises under 10% of student body. The structure varies from school-to-school, and fraternities/sororities may have their own houses or university housing.

Let's look at the benefits of going Greek:

1. **Friends** – I was Greek, and a large part of my motivation for going Greek was to meet people. As far as the "paying for friends" argument goes, I disagree. Dues pool resources to pay for activities, insurance, the house (on some campuses), etc.

2. **Activities** – You'll certainly be active on campus if you join a Greek organization. Fraternities and sororities participate in homecoming activities, have date parties, go on formals, and have social and philanthropic events throughout the year.

3. **Opportunities** – Many chapters have opportunities for scholarships, as do national organizations. You may also find internships and jobs through alumni (membership is indisputably good for networking).

4. **Social Skills** – You'll learn social skills. Regardless of what it may look like on the outside, fraternities and sororities have a lot of very different personalities who have to work together to make decisions that affect everyone.

Let's look at the downsides of being Greek:

1. **Cost** – It's expensive. Dues are expensive (liability insurance is nuts) as are the formals, t-shirts, memorabilia, membership pin, etc.

2. **Time Commitment** – This is somewhat dependent on you. Pledging is incredibly time intensive, but, in general, active

membership can be less involved. To a large extent, you decide your level of involvement.

3. **Alcohol & Drug Abuse** – Fraternity and sorority members are almost twice as likely to be binge drinkers. Illegal drug use (yes, weed counts) is more common in Greek life than the student population as a whole. The extent to which alcohol and drugs are problematic is incredibly. Some chapters and some colleges have few problems; other chapters and other colleges have very unhealthy, or even dangerous, environments. Alcohol/drug use during pledging is often a form of ritualized hazing, a particularly dangerous form.

4. **Hazing** – There is at least one hazing death per year on college campuses. Hazing is illegal and taken very seriously by colleges and universities. Unfortunately, it still exists and takes many forms: mental and emotional abuse, physical abuse, and substance abuse. If you're being hazed or involved in an organization that hazes, you need to report it to your university. Eventually, someone will be seriously hurt or killed, and you may face expulsion and felony charges.

Back to the original question, *should you join a fraternity or sorority?* It depends. While you'll influence the chapter you belong to, the chapter is likely to have a greater effect on you. My advice is to wait to rush (at least one semester) until you get a good feel for what the Greek organizations are like at your school. **Look at the members you meet and imagine what they'll be like in ten years. Then decide if that's the kind of person that you want to be.**

Student Government – You don't need political aspirations to get involved in student government, and it's a great way to pick up leadership skills and experience. You'll learn how to work with a big, unwieldy system (your college), and you'll learn how to come up with creative solutions (necessary in a big, unwieldy system). You'll make great connections within the university and its alumni. I strongly encourage you to check out student government and find something to get involved with—someone will be happy to put you on a committee or project. Believe it or not, your student government can make a real difference.

Intramurals – You'll find a ton of options for intramural participation from traditional sports to offerings like dodgeball and kickball. There are organized leagues, as well as pickup games. Even if you're not a great athlete, there's something for you. Intramurals are a great way to meet people, get some exercise, and have a good time.

Campus Media – Campus media is a wonderful way to get involved, particularly if you want to be a journalist or a content creator. You'll build a reel or portfolio that will be invaluable in applying for jobs or graduate school. In general, you have to "work your way up" in campus media. The really cool, important jobs will be given to juniors and seniors who have a few years of experience. You don't have to want to be a journalist or marketer to get involved. Campus publications are often ad supported, and business majors can both make money and get real-world experience selling ads.

Hazing Facts & Prevention	hazingprevention.org

11 ROOMMATES

Ah, roommates. There are good ones, bad ones, drunk ones, naked ones (shout out to Harlan Cohen's excellent book *The Naked Roommate*). Your relationship with your roommate can enhance your life or make you miserable. **Roommate trouble is a leading cause of students dropping out or transferring.**

It is absolutely imperative to sit down with your roommate as soon as possible and hammer out expectations. Setting expectations is vital, particularly if you have a prior relationship with your roommate. Whenever two (or more) people cohabitate, there will be conflicting values and preferences. Finding out the differences now is better than fighting about them later.

If you're living in the dorms, you'll probably have to write a roommate contract, where you set ground rules and discuss the possibility of RA intervention if you can't work out your differences. As corny as they sound, roommate contracts are a good idea—even in apartments, and they work if *all parties take them seriously*. I recommend that you augment that conversation, and make it clear that you take setting expectations seriously. In the Resources section, I've included a link to a legal version of a roommate question. It may be overkill for you or it may not. Regardless of how you want to set up your roommate agreement, here is a list of things to consider:

Belongings & Borrowing   Cleaning
Technology Use   Bills (Apartments)[*]
Overnight Romantic Guests   Smoking (apartments)

---

[*] Try and divide up the utilities so that the bills are about equal. You don't want your name on everything or nothing.

Overnight Non-Romantic Guests | Drinking/Drug Use
Party Hosting | Pets
Food | Toiletries
Household Necessities | Parking
Noise

How To Communicate

Be Direct – If something is bothering you, it's best to say it plainly and clearly. Do so in person, in private, and when you aren't mad. Joking about things sends the message that you aren't bothered. Being passive-aggressive makes people more stubborn and unwilling to change (they also may retaliate in their own passive-aggressive way).

Be Specific – Say what is wrong. "Please don't leave your dishes in the sink" is actionable, where "we need to keep a cleaner house" is not.

Use "I" Statements – To keep from accusing your roommate, or being perceived as accusing y our roommate, try using "I" statements. "I feel…" or "I need…." It comes off less preachy and confrontational than, "You need to…" or "You aren't…."

Listen – You've got to give your roommate room to complain without you reacting defensively or going on the attack.

General Roommate Advice

Address Problems Early – Your roommate, or roommates, will slip up or do something unintentionally. (By the way, so will you). If you don't address it early on, it will keep happening and you will begin to harbor resentment.

But Wait Until You're Not Annoyed – Wait until you can address your roommate calmly; otherwise, things will go poorly.

Be Patient – Nothing will be perfect, and you'll have to be more flexible than you probably expect. You'll have to let things go from time-to-time.

Pull the "See Ya Later" – Your roommate doesn't have to be your best friend. You don't always need to invite your roommate, nor should you expect them to invite you.

Talk in Person – If you have a problem with your roommate, don't address it by text. Intonation, sarcasm, and emotion are hard to convey in a text, and it's likely you'll end up escalating the issue into an argument.

Passive Aggressive Sucks – Don't be passive-aggressive. And if you find yourself on the receiving end of passive-aggressive behaviors, don't respond in kind.

If your roommate is passive aggressive, bring the issue out in the open, but don't accuse them of being passive-aggressive. Instead, say something like "I saw you did X, do you have an issue with what I'm doing about Y."

Standards Go Both Ways – Whatever you expect your roommate to do, you should already be doing. If you don't want dirty dishes in the sink, start by not leaving dirty dishes in the sink. Often, when people see a higher standard, they work towards it too.

Walk Away – If your roommate is driving you crazy, go somewhere else. It's not worth a war of stubbornness.

Remember It's Only a Year – You can get through this.

Off-Campus Advice

Living off-campus comes with additional issues. In addition to living with the person, you'll likely have to coordinate about guests, parking, utilities, housework, and rent. Here are some suggestions to keep everything easy and businesslike:

Divide up Chores & Set Rules – You can divide up the chores based on preference and that can work, and that works great for some people. For those of you less inclined, set general rules. For example, no dirty dishes left in the sink, smoking only outside, etc. I also recommend that you set aside a time to both clean your place.

Split the Bills – Only one of you will go on each utility, split them up. It's ideal if they add up to about the same for each of you. Post the bills or forward them by email as they come in and post or forward payment confirmations. Once the bills are paid, sort of who owes whom.

Parties/Gatherings – Set up how many times you want to have a sizeable party and how often it's OK just to have a few friends over. Also, make sure your bedroom door has a lock on it, both for privacy and to protect your stuff.

"Third" Roommate – Your roommate is in love, but all you got was another roommate. Set some boundaries on this by suggesting that they spend time at the significant other's place. In extreme cases, suggest that the significant other start paying rent or for some of the utilities.

If Talking Doesn't Work

Don't let a toxic relationship with a roommate compromise your academics or make you miserable. As mentioned at the top, roommate issues are one of the most frequently cited causes of transfers and dropouts. Work through your options, and keep in mind that it's just one year.

If you live in the dorms, talk to your RA. They can help mediate the issue. You aren't "telling on" your roommate, you are looking for a third party to mediate the dispute.

If the situation can't be resolved, you can switch rooms. Unless the situation is dire (involving harassment or abuse), it may take some time.

If you live off-campus, the burden is on you to resolve your roommate issues. It can be tough, both homework and dishes tend to pile up towards the end of the semester. Breaking a lease has serious consequences, so before you move out find out what your financial liability will be to your landlord (it also may affect your credit rating). In extreme cases, go ahead and do what you need to do.

Resources

The Naked Roommate	Harlan Cohen
Roommate Contract (legal)	www.lawdepot.com/contracts/roommate-agreement/

12 LIVING IN A DORM

Applying for Housing

Your housing application will be included in your admissions packet or as part of your school's web services. Review your options and **apply for housing as soon as possible**, housing assignments are made on a first come, first served basis. Uncertainty about your major and uncertainty about your roommate can make the issue more complicated. It can, at times, feel like there are a lot of moving parts.

If you're attending a large university, and you know what your major is (or are pretty sure) you may want to consider location. There are multiple layers to the housing decision: dorm selection, specialized floors, and rooms. You also have the additional layer of complexity of finding/selecting a roommate.

Different Styles of Housing (Advantages/Disadvantages)

Honors Dorms – Typically offer the best housing available to freshmen. The dorms tend to be well kept and well located, and the rooms tend to be nicer. There may be special facilities, trips, and resources available. Your peer group is likely to be more motivated, and more able to help, but they also may be more competitive. Most honors dorms are co-ed.

Disadvantage – Living in the honors dorm means participating in the honors program. I believe honors programs are worth it, but you can expect higher standards for GPA, additional work (for honors classes), and other demands on your time. If you have a specific roommate in mind, they will also need to be part of the honors program for you to room in honors housing. At many institutions, students can be a part of the honors program without living in the honors dorm.

Single-Sex Dorms – Are the most traditional setup for dorms, but they are becoming less and less common. From an educational standpoint, I don't see an advantage to single-sex dorms. (I don't think distraction is a credible argument). If you have religious or cultural problems with co-ed housing, then this may be your best option. Colleges with a strong religious affiliation tend to have *only* same-sex dorms.

Disadvantages – I think there are several disadvantages. Single-sex housing is often so limited that you may end up on a waiting list and, if offered a slot, you may have little to no input on your roommate. I also believe that self-selected single-sex housing can hinder you making broad and deep social connections. Rules about opposite sex visitation may be much stricter in single sex dorms. It's true that sexual activity and alcohol use are higher in co-ed dorms, but I don't believe you can say that co-ed dorms cause higher sexual activity and alcohol use. It may be that students who choose to live in single-sex housing are much less likely to engage in that behavior.

Co-Ed Dorms – I think that co-ed housing can improve your social skills. You get an idea of how "the other side lives" without the complexities of a romantic relationship. From an educational standpoint, I've found that students benefit from interacting with other genders, because of the differences in approach, organization, and perspective.

Disadvantages – You may feel like you need to dress well and act on your best behavior at all times, but this pressure usually fades quickly. There is a higher rate of sexual activity and alcohol use in co-ed dorms, but, again, I don't think that the co-ed living situation is the cause.

Co-ed Bathrooms – If your co-ed dorm has communal, AKA hallway, bathrooms, they may be either single-sex or co-ed. If the bathrooms are co-ed, they've been designed to protect your privacy while using the restroom or showering. That said, you're likely to be brushing your teeth next to someone of the opposite sex. Is it awkward at first? For some people it certainly is, but the awkwardness fades quickly.

Living Learning Communities – Vary quite a bit from college to college. They can be as simple as a grouping of freshmen on a floor who have the same major or expressed goals. On the other end, it can be a four-year, community experience where you take multiple classes with the same people, go on trips, participate in projects. In these more involved Living Learning Communities, you are essentially in a residential "college-within-a-college." (Check out the Chapter on *General Education Requirements* for more on the course aspects of Living Learning Communities).

From an educational standpoint, living-learning communities offer some great advantages. They enhance your experience and provide excellent opportunities. Students participating in living-learning communities have higher major GPA's and higher graduation rates.

Disadvantages – You may be limiting whom you meet by living with and taking classes with the same people. One of the more valuable aspects of college is interacting and understanding those with different backgrounds, majors, interests, and beliefs. If you're in a very involved living-learning community, getting involved in non-major related activities and organizations is more important. If you have a specific roommate in mind, they'll need to be a part of the living-learning community to be able to live in that dorm or on that floor.

Gender-Neutral Housing – In gender-neutral housing, students often have roommates of the opposite sex. Gender-neutral housing is a relatively recent development; the goal is to create healthy, safe environments for LGBTQ students. Access to gender-neutral housing may require you to be transgender or gender non-conforming. Some colleges/universities allow any student to request gender-neutral housing.

These housing arrangements are often a collaborative venture between the university and the LGBTQ organization(s) on campus. LGBTQ students report feeling safer and more accepted in gender-neutral housing. They have lower rates of depression, higher grades, and higher graduation rates.

Rooms, Suites, & Apartments

Suites – are two or more rooms that share a bathroom, and sometimes a living room. You get more privacy and more space. You also share your bathroom with only a few people. A semi-suite is roughly the same, except you don't have a living room. You may or may not have a roommate in your bedroom.

Disadvantages – You'll still need to keep your bathroom supplies in your room—I guarantee you they will be used otherwise. You may be partially responsible for keeping the bathroom and common/living room clean.

Rooms – are what you picture when you think of a dorm room. They can be singles, doubles, triples, or even quads. Most colleges/universities have very limited singles, particularly for freshmen. As such, you'll probably be living with at least one other person. If you're disappointed by that, let me assure you it's for the best. Aside from expanding your social network, you'll also learn a lot about how to live with someone, how to deal with disagreements, and how to manage a relationship. You're not done with roommates after freshmen year, so starting to develop these skills doesn't hurt.

Disadvantages – You have little personal space or privacy. For more on dealing with a roommate, check out the preceding chapter on *Roommates*.

Apartments – College/University run apartments are typically reserved for upper-classmen or upper-class transfer students. In addition to a private bathroom and living room, these apartments usually have a full kitchen.

Disadvantages – You'll end up having the same problems as living in an apartment (except utility bills). It can be complicated by the fact that your roommate (if you're a transfer) may be randomly assigned. You'll have to figure out the standard issues: don't eat my food, how are we going to keep the place clean, how loud can you play music/tv, etc.

13 THE CORE OF SUCCESS
Who Succeeds, Resilience, Perfectionism, & Procrastination

Thriving & Failure to Thrive

You've heard this story before: *so-and-so* was a brilliant student in high school, they couldn't get a B if they tried, got a full ride to Awesome U, but two years later they failed out and were living in their parents' basement. You've also heard this story: *what's her name* was a real wreck in high school, her grades weren't great, and she partied all the time, but she just got accepted to medical school.

What happened? Why did *so-and-so* fail to thrive while *what's her name* exceeded all expectations? There isn't one answer, even for my hypothetical students. People are complicated and a lot of factors are probably at work.

It's somewhat likely that the young man who crashed and burned had some mental health issues that went unaddressed (please read the chapter on *Mental Health*, it's more likely to be relevant to you than you think). It's also likely that he was unaccustomed to even the possibility of failure. He took his position for granted, and did not believe that anything bad could or would happen to him.

So-and-so on the other hand either had a skill set and a motivation that was invisible to outsiders until now, or she matured and went after a very specific goal.

But the more useful answer is that *so-and-so* likely lacked some of the soft skills necessary for success in college while *what's her name* did not.

Success in college is different than success high school. You have to be self-motivated, organized, and make good use of your time. College classes are different, harder, and there is more work than classes in high school. At the same time, you have to fend for yourself.

I address different parts of the failure to thrive problem throughout the book. This section will focus on the soft-skills of organization, time management, habit formation, goal setting, and self-starting. Please check out the chapters on *Building a Healthy Life*, *Building Academic Success*, and *How to Graduate in Four Years*.

Resilience: The Most Important Character Trait

Bouncing back is the most important personal trait you can develop. Sooner or later, bad things—even catastrophic things—will happen to you. It's inevitable, and it's outside your control. How you respond to setbacks is what matters.

I discuss academic setbacks in the chapter on *Bad Test, Bad Class, Bad Semester*. The advice in that chapter works for all setbacks from breakups to deaths.

Life is hard sometimes, and it's seldom fair. You don't need to be tougher than life; that's foolish advice, and I wince when I hear it. It's also not about avoiding bad blows; you can't. **It's all about getting back up**. I strongly recommend Angela Duckworth's fantastic book *Grit: The Power of Passion & Perseverance*. There are some other great resources listed in this chapter and at the end of *Bad Test, Bad Class, Bad Semester*.

Perfectionism is Your Enemy

Uncontrolled, undirected perfectionism is your enemy. You cannot win. Get a 98? You should have gotten a 100. Got a 100? You're probably going to fail the lab report you just turned in. There's no room for success and no room to enjoy success. Because you can't exceed your aims, you can only disappoint yourself, and carry a relentless psychological burden. In the resources section of this chapter, you'll find a link to the multidimensional perfectionism index. It's not meant to diagnose you, but it can help you assess and think about your relationship with perfectionism.

Here are my recommendations for dealing with unhealthy perfectionism.

1. **Set Realistic Goals** – I think the *Goal Setting* chapter is one of the, most important chapters in this book. Setting healthy, realistic, and

manageable goals will allow you to measure yourself without "shifting the goal posts". For perfectionists, it's incredibly important that you have a positive relationship with goals, one where you feel inspired and not anxious.

2. **Prioritize** – Don't get caught up in little details. Focus on the big picture on bigger projects and in test prep.

3. **Get Going** – If you find your perfectionism paralyzing, just try and get going. Have what the U.S. Marines call "a bias towards action". If you absolutely can't get going, I recommend you see a counselor (see the chapter on *Mental Health*).

4. **Celebrate** – Take time and celebrate *every* small victory, even if your celebration is doing something that you want to do for a half an hour. Relish in the accomplishment. It's very important that you learn to appreciate what you've done, not "how much better it could have been".

5. **Move On** – Mourn your failures but not for very long. Move on, and use them as positive life lessons.

6. **Take Care of Yourself** – Exercise, eat right, sleep, and make sure you're emotionally OK. It's unsustainable to live unreasonably. Not only will it hurt you, it will also hurt your long-term success.

Procrastination

It may seem that perfectionism and procrastination are opposite sides of the same coin. In fact, however, the two are often linked. It may come as no surprise, but procrastination is correlated with low test scores, paper/project scores, and GPA. Here are some causes of procrastination:

1. **I'm afraid to fail.** Fear of failure is paralyzing. You don't know how to get started, and you're overly critical of any actions you take. You constantly grade yourself by the harshest rubric, and, guess what? You fail to live up. Studying and coursework becomes a wholly negative experience (it's not usually fun to begin with) when you deride yourself the entire time. You also, ironically, impair your own performance—you end up doing worse than if you had been charitable to yourself.

What to do: Check out the list on the previous page about perfectionism. Make sure you're living a healthy and balanced life. Most of all, make sure you're engaging in positive goal setting.

2. **I'm afraid my work won't be perfect.** The bad (and good news) is that your work won't and shouldn't be perfect. You're in college to learn and develop skills. Aside from the economic necessity of a degree, you are in college to get an education. If you were already capable of acing every course with little effort, you'd be wasting your time (and a whole bunch of money).

   What to do: Check your expectations a little. It's a wonderful thing to have incredibly high aspirations, and, frankly, the educational climate today fosters that. But high aspirations without concrete, achievable goals will make you an anxious, unhappy mess. Engage in positive goal setting, prioritize, use time management skills, and break large tasks into small ones.

3. **I don't know how to get started.** Often this means you doubt your abilities. Start by breaking a huge task down into manageable components. Remember, you can only chew in bite-sized pieces. It may also be that you're not used to academic settings where the teacher does not walk you through every step of a large project (most US high schools do a fair amount of handholding).

   What to do: It's likely you have most of the skills, to one degree or another, so break your project down. If you're having trouble, use the resources provided by your school (check out the chapter on *Tests & Assignments*).

4. **I'm afraid of success.** Fear of success is somewhat more common in graduate students than undergrads, but it can affect anyone. Usually fear of success means that you'll create the impression in others that you're "better" than you are. People who fear success often believe that they'll never be able to live up to a "fluke" performance and will be considered "frauds" or worse that people will discover that they were never talented.

What to do: Think about this rationally: if you're good enough to succeed once, you're good enough to do it again. I don't buy that people were "lucky" if they got a great grade on a major project or a big exam. Luck may win you a coin toss, or under extraordinary circumstances 10 coin tosses in a row, but it won't write a killer paper for you. I'm no psychologist, but it's my pet theory that people who end up as "flukes" either become complacent or they have some issue dealing with success (maybe paralyzed by the fear that they will become flukes).

5. **I work best under pressure/like it.** Research doesn't support the notion that people actually "enjoy" the pressure when they're under it. They merely romanticize it before or after the event. Further, a sizable meta-study indicates that people who claim to work best under pressure actually don't. There appears to be a cognitive bias here, where students remember the instance(s) where it worked out great, but not the much more frequent instances where it didn't. Philosophers would call this the fallacy of misleading vividness (it's cool and important, look it up).

   What to do: Start by making a list of all the times you procrastinated. Close your eyes and remember how it felt the night before or the morning of the deadline. Does it seem exciting in retrospect? Now, review the grades (approximate is good enough) you got on those projects/tests. Do you really believe that you got the best grade you could have gotten? What if you had taken more time and spread out the assignment?

   If you agree that procrastination isn't helping you, then start by implementing an effective time management system (check out the chapter on *Time Management*). Also, make sure you're engaging in positive goal setting.

6. **I have this habit, and I can't change it.** When other people say this, it sounds like an excuse. When it's your habit and your life, it doesn't feel like one. Habits are difficult to change (otherwise they wouldn't be habits). Not only are they hard to change, but it takes a long time for that change to stick.

What to do: The fact that you recognize that you have this habit and acknowledge that it's going to be difficult to change is an excellent first step. You'll need to hack your brain, creating a new reward and cue system. Check out the chapter on *Habit Formation* for some actionable advice.

7. **It doesn't matter/I don't care/no one cares.** Apathy is often a disguise for a fear of failure or a fear of success. I guarantee that it matters, you're getting a grade. I also guarantee that others care, not just the people in your life but your professors as well. And, I guarantee you that you care. If you didn't care, you wouldn't be reading this right now. Gotcha!

What to do: Try and figure out what's going on. Are you doubting your ability to succeed, or are you afraid of the consequences if you do succeed? Or are you unhappy where you are or with what you're studying? Life is a big place, and there's as much adventure in it as you're willing to take. Figure out why you think you don't care, and then work to address that problem.

In This Section

Habit Formation – A surprising percentage of our daily activities are habitual. I give an overview on how habits work, how to break bad habits, and how to establish good habits.

Goal Setting – Formal goal setting is an activity that will trickle through your life in a positive way. I cannot recommend it strongly enough, no matter if you're a procrastinator, a perfectionist, or somewhere in between. I think it's one of the most important chapters in the book.

Organization – Formal goal setting is an activity that will trickle through your life in a positive way. I cannot recommend it enough if you're a procrastinator, a perfectionist, or somewhere in between.

Time Management & Self Starting – Making effective use of your time is harder than ever, given the ease and frequency with which we are distracted. Learn some strategies to manage your time well so you can have a less stressful, more successful, and more fun life.

Resources

Grit: The Power of Passion & Perseverance	Angela Duckworth
The Road to Resilience APA	apa.org/helpcenter/road-resilience.aspx
The Procrastination Cure…	Damon Zahariades
Perfectionism Test	psychologytoday.com/us/tests/personality/ perfectionism-test

14 CREATE GREAT HABITS

You are Already a Creature of Habit

Up to 40% of our daily activities are habitual. We establish habits to achieve a goal or reward, and, for the most part, we do so unintentionally. In general, habits operate outside of our conscious awareness. College is a wonderful time to establish new habits as your surroundings, daily activities, and peer group will be radically different. Even if you aren't just entering your freshmen year, college is full of new beginnings, every semester or year is a fresh chance to start all over.

In the resources section of this chapter, you'll find Charles Duhigg's excellent book, *The Power of Habit*. I strongly recommend it as a resource for how to quit bad habits and how to create good habits. In fact, this has been a difficult chapter to write, as Mr. Duhigg's book is so excellent and comprehensive that it's hard not to rip him off.

How Habits Work

Habits are cyclical. A *trigger* starts the cycle. The trigger causes you to *act*. That action results in a *reward* (even if it's not good for you). The reward keeps you returning to the habit. The reward and the unconscious nature of habits make them difficult to start and even more difficult to break.

Master Your Habits or They Will Master You

Habits operate "behind our backs", so the first step is to identify what habits you have that you'd like changed or what habits you'd like to start. In either case, the key is figuring out what triggers the habit and what reward you get from the habit. You can have multiple triggers and multiple rewards for the same habit.

Let's say you're a smoker for example. You could be triggered by finishing a meal, leaving class, needing a break, a craving for nicotine, or even use cigarettes as a social crutch. Your rewards include the nicotine, taking a break, a conversation starter, and a change in scenery.

It's often said that it takes 21 days to establish a new habit, but there's not much science behind that number. **If you want to establish a new habit or break an old one, expect it to take much longer—at least two months and up to one year.** So the next time you find yourself still struggling to not smoke or to go to the gym, after a few weeks of excellent behavior, remind yourself that habits aren't formed or broken in only a few weeks.

It takes time. You will mess up. Don't quit or fall back in completely. It is a chore to break an old habit or establish a new habit, but it will be worth it in the end.

The Role of Willpower

Willpower takes a lot of energy. As such, changing habits is far better than an abrupt cessation and "white knuckling" your way through.

No one sets out to lose 10 pounds in the hopes of gaining it back, but it happens all the time. When you lapse out of good habits or back into bad habits, it's often because you've been running on willpower the whole time, instead of creating a new reward sequence that makes the habit self-sustaining.

By-in-large, we do the things we want to do. As someone who is self-employed, I can attest that while I spend most of my day working, I often duck tasks that I'm unsure about or I feel stuck on (like this chapter). It's easy because I don't have anyone to answer to.

While people are complex, I think you can boil down motivations into either sticks or carrots. I don't have an external stick (I can't fire myself), so I focus on carrots. I'll survive, for example, if this book never came out. I have to remind myself that I think this book can help people, how accomplished I felt when I released my first book, and that I will hopefully make a few bucks by finishing it.

But that's not enough to get me to write this particular chapter. So instead, I'm focusing on how good I'll feel when I have the first draft of this chapter, how I won't have that lingering doubt/anxiety about this material, and how I'll be able to move on to other parts of the book will be easier to work on. So, while I still don't want to write this chapter, I want the reward of *having written* this chapter. So, I'm using a little willpower to achieve this goal.

Establishing Good Habits

It's all about the trigger and the reward. You need to establish a trigger to prompt you to begin the action sequence of the habit. For example, if you want to create a habit of going to the library every day, start walking there directly after a class or pack your bag before class with the materials you'll need at the library. Do this every day, and before too long you'll be on autopilot. There are a host of apps on the market that can help you track good habits and break bad ones.

The trigger may prompt the action, but it alone is insufficient to build durable habits. You need to have a reward. For example, if you go to the library, maybe you treat yourself to a coffee or treat. You can also make the reward accomplishment based, by "stopping to smell the roses." Focus on that feeling of productivity and control that you have after your library visit.

Accomplishment rewards work best if they're coupled with some activity. For me, it's ticking items off my to-do list. For you, it may be logging your progress off your study plan for an exam. I strongly encourage you to do something to reward yourself that ties the habit into your goal framework— it's incredibly helpful to remember *why* you do things.

Remember that habits are not the same as goals. Habits can serve the purpose of goals, but habits are small, automatic behaviors.

To establish good habits, you need to tie new triggers into behaviors. The closer the trigger, the action, and the reward are, the more successful you will be.

1. **Identify the habit** – Start small with your habits, the smaller a habit is, the easier it is to institute (and the more staying power it has). Whatever the habit is, you'll need to be committed to doing it. If you aren't committed, save it for later. You'll frustrate yourself and make no progress unless you have a strong intention to act.

2. **Identify the triggers** – What will cue you to act? Good triggers are linked with behaviors you do automatically already, and they remove an impediment from acting. For example, if you set your gym clothes out, or pack your gym bag, that's one less thing to keep you from the gym.

3. **Identify the reward(s)** – Rewards are both long term and short term, but to truly establish a habit, focus on short-term rewards.

Getting in great shape is a reward, but it won't be enough to get you to the gym regularly. Each time you do the activity there needs to be a reward. Don't be afraid to treat yourself if it makes it easier to ease into the habit. You can later decide whether to replace the habit of that reward.

4. **Anticipate Obstacles** – You won't always want to go to the gym, the library, or do whatever new activity you have in mind. You'll have bad days. Do your best to keep up with your habits, but expect that life will resist you at times.

5. **Implement** – Jump in feet first. When the trigger happens, immediately engage in the action that leads to the reward. The closer the link between the cue and the reward, the more likely you are to form a durable habit.

6. **Adjust** – You won't be perfect; you'll have to use trial and error and be patient with yourself.

Banishing Bad Habits

Stopping bad habits doesn't work well, but you can **replace bad habits**. It's hard to quit a bad habit because you're hooked on the reward the bad habit provides.

I used to drink way too much diet soda. I knew it was a bad habit, but I liked soda, and, as the parent of a small, irascible child, the caffeine didn't hurt. I even liked to walk to the little convenience store to buy soda.

There are a few triggers in the soda habit. I felt tired, or I felt like I needed a little extra umph. Sometimes, I felt stressed (stress and boredom are major triggers for bad habits). Or maybe I just want to go outside, but I felt like I needed a "mission" or my time wouldn't be spent productively.

If I wanted to replace diet soda, I need to replace the triggers and the rewards.

To start, I tried drinking tea instead of soda. That worked somewhat, but I'm not crazy about tea, and it's certainly not fizzy or artificially sweet. While, in time, a straight tea replacement would work, it wasn't a good replacement habit. So, I changed my morning routine to include more activity before I started working. That helped too, as it alleviated the cue of wanting to get out and do something. I also started drinking seltzer water. Finally, I took the money I saved (teabags and seltzer are cheaper than pop) and used it to buy myself something each month.

By identifying the cues which were closely tied to the rewards, I was able to cut back on my diet soda consumption. I still walk to the convenience store, from time to time, and buy a soda. In fact, I'm drinking one right now. But I don't mind so much as I've largely replaced that activity. It's not about being perfect, it's about killing the automatic cycle.

Remember, **breaking bad habits is all about replacing them with good habits.** To banish bad habits follow the following steps:

1. **Identify the habit**

2. **Identify the triggers** – What cues the behavior pattern? Do you always smoke as soon as you leave class? You can't quit going to class, but you could substitute smoking with something enjoyable.

3. **Identify the reward(s)** – Be careful, rewards aren't always what you think they are. Smoking a cigarette with your roommate may be an excuse to take a break and chat for 10 minutes and that reward may be stronger than the allure of nicotine.

4. **Come up with an alternative or alternatives that replace the reward** – Your alternatives need to scratch the same itch, and you may need to adjust your rewards. Sometimes, we aren't clear on what the rewards are when we try to break or establish a habit.

5. **Implement** – Jump in feet first. The most important thing is to do the new habit whenever you would have been triggered by the old cue.

6. **Adjust** – This won't be perfect at first, you'll have to use trial and error and be patient with yourself. Don't expect perfection.

What Makes a Good Cue?

Whether you're trying to implement a new habit or replace a bad habit, the strength of your cue is of paramount importance. Here's what makes a good cue:

✓ It's tied into something you already do automatically (another habit) *or* you are cued automatically (a phone reminder).

✓ It's tied into something that will happen to you regardless. For example, your Tuesday morning lecture ends.

✓ It's either a reminder or an easily accomplished first step.

- ✓ It allows you to get in the mindset of the actions required to complete the habit.
- ✓ Your concrete environment matters more than your abstract motivation. Visual or physical cues will be a lot more effective than nagging self-reminders.
- ✓ Fit things in your day. You can use habits to gradually restructure your life, but you'll be far more successful if you integrate your habits into the existing structure of your day and change things piece by piece.

What Makes a Good Reward?

Good rewards are rewarding. They should also be about the same magnitude as the habit itself. For example, if you eat a salad for lunch minutes, a family sized bag of chips is not a proportionate reward. There's another issue there, I'm not opposed to treating yourself, but watch rewards that are contrary to the goal of the habit you are forming.

Resources

The Power of Habit: Why we Do What We Do in Life & Business	Charles Duhigg
Tiny Habits (Stanford)	tinyhabits.com
HabitBull*	Apple & Android App Store

*There are quite a few habit apps on the market, each somewhat different. Personally, I like HabitBull, but do some research and think about what will fit you best.

15 SET GOALS

The Importance of Goal Setting

Research has consistently shown that goal setting improves grades and self-reported well-being (happiness/satisfaction). Setting goals increases your control and autonomy over your education and life, boosts your motivation, and makes you more likely to take reasonable risks and demonstrate perseverance. Healthy risk-taking and perseverance and have an enormous positive impact on your life.

There's a concept in psychology called the *locus of control*, a spectrum of how much control people believe that they have over their lives. People with an *internal locus of control* believe they have a high degree of control over their life. People with an *external locus of control* believe that external factors determine what happens in their lives. Most people are somewhere in the middle. It's likely that you have an internal locus of control on some issues and an external on others.

People with an internal locus of control don't believe they are the master of the universe and all that happens within; it only means that they believe they have a *major* impact on what happens to them and how their life turns out. When you have an internal locus of control, you put the responsibility to succeed on yourself. Research has repeatedly shown that people with an internal locus of control are more successful and are physically and mentally healthier. The good news, you can develop an internal locus of control.

How to develop an internal locus of control – To start with, set goals. Follow through on those goals using organizational and time management principles. There's no teacher better than experience, and by taking control (insomuch as possible), you'll learn how a solid perspective and a proactive attitude will improve the quality of your life.

My Goal Philosophy

1. **Setting and pursuing goals needs to be a positive experience**. You have to look at what you're doing well, where you can improve and use setbacks as a way to ensure future attempts go better. Try and focus on goals that make you grow, whether as a person or towards a profession. Try not to use goals where the aim is to avoid a negative consequence or maintain the status quo.

2. **Don't expect perfection.** You're a person, not a machine. You'll make mistakes, and things will go wrong. Focus on the process of achieving goals, and the process of using goal setting and related skills to help you develop.

3. **You can't do everything.** It took me a long time to learn this one, but you can only become an expert on one or two subjects. You can enjoy multiple hobbies, but be deeply involved in one or two. By actively deciding what you want to be great at, you will be more comfortable with what you don't know or do as well.

4. **You should have both _exploratory_ and _focused_ goals.** Exploratory goals force you into novel situations and experiences. Exploratory goals help you discover who you are as a person and what is important to you. Focused goals move you towards a particular career path and lifestyle. I think that balancing your goals between these two domains is incredibly important at any stage of life.

5. **Failure doesn't mean failure.** If making mistakes doesn't mean you failed, then failure doesn't make you a failure. The best lessons in life are learned when things go jarringly wrong. Remember, failure is never final, and defeat is never permanent.

Goal Types

Don't just set goals for your career or your education, set goals in multiple areas of your life. People who lead a well-balanced life, with a variety of goals, are more satisfied and more successful. That said, longer-term goals can seem insurmountable and, as such, can lower your happiness. The key is to focus on the short and medium term goals (termed this week and this semester, respectively) and use the long-term (undergraduate goals) and life-long goals to remind yourself why you're doing all this to begin with.

Educational Educational and career goals have significant overlap. At a base level, your educational goals are to get good grades and earn a degree in your major or majors (although double majoring typically doesn't add a lot of value for you, check out the chapter on *Majors* for more). You may add other goals that are more loosely connected: foreign language proficiency, learning JAVA, completing a minor, working in a research lab, etc. A good example of a goal that overlaps the domains of educational and career is earning admission into a graduate or professional program.

Career Career goals could be a type of job or employer like working for an investment bank. But career goals will also encompass stepping-stone goals, like nailing an internship in banking or conducting research that makes you attractive to employers.

Wellbeing We overlook wellbeing, and tell ourselves that there's always time later. But taking care of yourself is the first step to taking care of everything else. If you're 18, or 22, or 25, you bounce back relatively quickly, but that will slow as you age, and your habits will be harder to change. Eat reasonably healthy, get regular exercise, and take care of your mental health.

Wellbeing goals are not all about staying healthy, they're also about personal development. Listen to podcasts, read books, and spend time with people who matter.

You may have a long-term goal of running a marathon, and a medium-term goal of completing a 5k. You could also have a goal to spend more time with your family, friends, your faith, or involved in a club. If you're having issues, a short-term goal can be to make and keep an appointment with your school's mental health services (check out the chapter on *Mental Health*).

Personal Development These can be tough goals to set because they are hard to quantify. If you have low confidence, start there. Confidence, grit (AKA perseverance), and organization are more important for success than IQ. In the following chapters, I discuss how to become more organized.

Milestones Milestone goals are typically undergraduate goals or long-term goals. They include graduating (or graduating with some distinction), earning admission to a graduate/professional program or being hired to a dream job (or the prelude to a dream job), home ownership, having children, starting a business, etc.

Goal Duration

You'll find that the timeframe I suggest is different from most goal setting literature. I've done this for a couple reasons. One, it's probably your first experience with formal goal setting and I want you to have early successes; college is divided into semesters, trimesters, or quarters, which create natural breaks and the culmination of the effort of a time period. Two, your life as an undergraduate will be very different from your life in the workforce or in graduate school, so I feel it makes sense to punctuate this part of your life.

Short-Term Goals – What are your goals for this week? If it's to ace your biology lab quiz, then you'll have a concrete, achievable goal that you can break into individual steps or tasks. Do you want to go to the gym three times this week (maybe as part of a larger goal of losing your freshman 15)? That can be broken into three small goals for the week.

Medium-Term Goals – What are you trying to accomplish this semester? Do you want to make the Dean's list? If so, you can break your coursework, and the relative difficulty of your classes down, so that you have an idea of what it will take.

Undergraduate Goals – The next four (or less) years will result in what? Admission to dental school, a job as a consultant, admission to a doctoral program? These are the apex goals of your time as an undergrad, but don't be too restrictive. Getting into Harvard Law School is a laudable aspiration, but it is probably too restrictive as a goal. It may be better to have a goal like, "get into a top-10 law school." These goals shouldn't be wholly career and education oriented; you may have a goal to speak fluent Spanish, run an ultra-marathon, or publish an original piece of writing or research.

Long-Term Goals – These will, likely, change the most. You may be dead set against having children but change your mind. You may want to live in Chicago, try it out a few years, then move to Boston. You may want to design aircraft for a living, but end up working for SpaceX. Life will take you in funny directions. Long-term goals should be the loosest, most qualitative goals. Be careful not to interpret these too strictly and shutter yourself from interesting opportunities.

Creating Good Goals

Control – There are very few goals that you'll have *total* control over. But you should be able to exert significant influence on your goals.

Bad Goal – "Start dating the cute surfer guy down the hall."

You can't control whether the cute surfer guy is interested or whether he is currently involved. You can definitely take a shot, but he's in control of how he feels about you.

Better Goal – "Start casually dating."

This is something you can control. You can find people who like spending time with you, and are interested in investigating the potential for a romantic relationship. Notice that this goal is less specific but more within your control.

Positive – Goals should be stated positively, as achievements, not as warnings.

Bad Goal – "Don't F up my accounting final."

Even if you do great on your accounting final, the best you can say about yourself is that you aren't a complete loser.

Better Goal – "Get an X on my accounting final."

This is something you can shoot for. If you need an A to get an A in the class, then shoot for the A. With the specific knowledge of what you need, you'll know how to structure your study time. Goal setting is a great time to play trade-offs. If you only need a B to maintain your A, then you can take a little of the time from preparing for the accounting final and put it elsewhere.

Committed – Only set goals that you are committed to. Goal setting will be frustrating and depressing if you set a bunch of goals you're only loosely attached to. You're unlikely to achieve goals that you don't want enough. A warning sign of loose-attachment to goals is having a lot of goals, particularly if they have some conflict. A good way to test your commitment is the "pain test". Are you willing to go through the difficulties of achieving the goal? Is the end result worth the journey?

Bad Goal – "I hate running, but I want to get in better shape so I'll train for a 10k."

I only run from bears and my ex, so this would be a terrible goal for me. Fortunately, there are a lot of ways to get or stay in shape, so I don't have to run. Often, we choose goals that we aren't committed to because we don't consider alternative routes to the same destination (getting in shape in the 10k example). **Beware of being a martyr; there is a subset of people who believe the worse the experience, the better the result.** (I have an uncle who seems to believe that the worse something tastes, the better it is for you). Meaningful goals are challenging, but they shouldn't be miserable.

Better Goal – "I want to get in better shape, so I'll try different exercise classes and gym routines until I find what I like to do."

This is a very solid goal. It's exploratory and shows commitment. A good short-term version of this goal would be "try a yoga class this week, and a weight workout next." The goals that don't make you miserable are the goals you stick with. In fact, using running again (I have nothing against it, it's just not for me) people who get in shape by training for a marathon are statistically unlikely to keep up their exercise after they run their marathon.

Specific – Goals need to be specific. Otherwise, you can't make a concrete plan to achieve the goal or measure yourself against the goal to evaluate progress. (Goals can be too specific, however, as we saw in the *Control* example.)

Bad Goal – "I'm going to get good grades this semester."

How do you qualify good grades? It's not specific enough, and, for most of you, one of two things will happen. You'll decide your grades weren't good enough, or you'll decide your grades were pretty good, all things considered. Either way you're cheating yourself out a measuring stick that could have improved your performance in the immediate and helped you evaluate how to improve your performance for the future.

Better Goal – "I'm going to get a 3.5 GPA this semester."

That's a solid goal, with several paths to achieving it. It's got a time frame, and it's specific enough to allow you to create smaller goals to aid in your organization and time management. It's also an easy goal to check in on. You can look at your grades at any point and see if you're on track to earn that spot on the Dean's List (3.5 or better at most schools).

Challenging – You shouldn't hit every single one of your goals. If you are, you're setting them too low. Instead, expect that you'll fall short on a reasonable percentage. Personally, I think 20 – 30% is good, although traditional OKR methodology (discussed below) suggests 50%. But remember that challenging does not mean impossible. It's a bit paradoxical, but very challenging goals can be easier to achieve than simple goals because harder goals are more motivating and get more attention.

Bad Goal – "I'm going to pass all of my classes this semester."

This goal has two problems, it doesn't define pass (technically a D is passing, but you may be required to repeat the course) and it's a low bar.

Instead of inspiring you, this goal may become an excuse to be complacent.

Better Goal – "I'm going to get A's in my major classes, and at least a B in my math course."

This is a good goal for someone who struggles with Math. They set an attainable goal for themselves, while also recognizing the importance of keeping up their GPA, particularly in regard to classes within their major.

Bad Goal 2 – "I'm going to become a Rhodes Scholar."

Being a Rhodes scholar is a laudable goal, but this goal falls short on two fronts. One, it's significantly outside of your control—the Rhodes scholarship is one of the most competitive scholarships in the world. Two, The goal is so lofty that a single misstep could be incredibly discouraging.

Better Goal 2 – "I'm going to be a serious candidate to become a Rhodes Scholar."

This goal fixes the control problem by implicitly acknowledging that all you can do is put your best foot forward. It also fixes the lofty aspect in the same manner. Additionally, it is easier to digest, as you can find out what a good Rhodes Scholarship candidate has on their resume and set goals to emulate it.

Time Table – As a student, a lot of your goals will automatically have timetables because of the episodic nature of college. Longer-term goals may not.

Bad Goal – "I'm going to own my own home by age 30."

On the surface, this is a pretty reasonable goal. Harder to achieve, perhaps, than in the past, but a reasonable goal nonetheless. It can be broken into smaller, categorical goals like building and maintaining a good credit score and saving money for a down payment. But it fails to account for all the vagaries of life. Perhaps you decide to change careers or pursue a graduate degree at a later date. You have a child and put off home ownership until you can recoup the costs. Or, you may not be happy in your current location and be considering a move across the country. As silly as it sounds, once you've had that goal for a long time, even a valid reason for postponing it can make you feel like a failure.

Better Goal – "I'm going to be in a position to own a home by age 30."

This seemingly small change makes a drastic impact on the goal. It requires that you engage in the meaningful components of the goal (good credit score & savings) without penning you in.

Bad Goal – "I'm going to get in awesome shape."

There's no timetable here, so, conceivably you could get in "awesome shape" when you're 80. There's also no concrete aspect to it, so the definition of awesome shape is too loose. This is more of an objective (as in OKR methodology) than a goal.

Better Goal – "I'm going to go to the gym three times a week this semester to train for a half-marathon in May."

This is specific, it has a timetable, and it has a clear objective that you'll have to train towards.

Goal Setting Tools

Write Your Goals Down – I believe that goal setting does not work unless you write your goals down where you will see them every day. You can post them on your wall above your desk, or, if that's too embarrassing, make multiple copies on the inside cover of your notebooks. Read them daily. It's a motivational check-in. If it becomes depressing or defeating to look at your goals, you're not breaking your goals into small enough chunks, not using failure to inform future success (see the chapter *Bad Test. Bad Class, Bad Semester* for more), or you weren't that committed to your goals to begin with.

Prioritize – It's essential to prioritize goals when they come into conflict. If you're feeling iffy about tomorrow's history midterm and you have an intramural game today, you'll need to prioritize the midterm over the game, even if your goals conflict. Competing in intramural can be a semester goal for a longer-term goal (or objective in OKR), but there will be many intramural games and only one history midterm.

You can't be the best at everything, so some things come to the forefront and some things slip behind. If you're doing a good job staying ahead in your classes (check out the *Organization* and *Time Management* chapters), you shouldn't be navigating crisis to crisis. I like to prioritize goals from the top-down. Decide what your most important long-term goal is and then prioritize the medium-term goals that support it, and then the short-term goals that support the medium term goals. Prioritization is absolutely critical in school and in the workplace. Otherwise, you'll end up spending a lot of time on a lot of things that yield very little (have trouble saying "no"? check out the chapter on *Getting Involved*). **It's the deep focus, the lasting effort that produces results that change your life.**

Track – Through the use of frequent small goals, you can keep track of your progress towards your semester and long-term goals. Research indicates that tracking goals improves your well-being and happiness. That makes sense, tracking goals that are going well is like a mini-celebration, tracking goals that are going poorly helps you to identify and address the problem. The feeling that you're floundering—just keeping your head above water—is absolutely terrible. Feeling as though life is unmanageable happens when you aren't sure what's going wrong or how to correct it. Tracking keeps you on course, minimizes "detours", and allows you to identify and address problems quickly and calmly.

There are several methods for tracking goals, but you need to do it formally. I like setting aside the same time every week—use your calendar—to have a short meeting with yourself and evaluate what worked and didn't work this past week. When you start, you may want to track daily or twice a week. It's vital to keep a positive attitude when you evaluate yourself. Congratulate yourself on what went well, and be accountable for what didn't. **Accountability does not mean beating yourself up.**

Goal Setting Systems
Goal setting systems are like the steering wheel in a car: they determine direction. The subsequent chapters (habit formation, self-starting, organization, time management, and study skills) are the engine that drives you toward your goals. I introduced my goal setting system above, and below I discuss other popular options. **Ultimately, the best goal setting system is the one you'll use.**

S.M.A.R.T. Goal Setting

SMART is the most popular goal setting system; in fact, your college may have already introduced it to you. There are a ton of variations on the acronym, and, if SMART is attractive to you, google the acronyms and see which one you like best. The following is just one of many options:

Specific –   Goals need to be specific so they may be tracked and measured.

Measurable –   You have to be able to measure by either yes/no or by degree your progress or success/failure with the goal.

Achievable –   You have a reasonable likelihood of success. This does not mean, however, that success is a given.

Realistic –   The goal isn't only achievable, it is realistic that you will put the time and effort in to achieve the goal.

Timetable –   You need a timetable to create a sense of urgency, so if one is not defined for you, for example, by the length of a semester, define it for yourself.

I like this system, the system I introduced earlier is somewhat inspired by it. The only addition I would make is to ensure that you have *exploratory* goals listed.

Critics allege that the SMART framework can make you play life too safe. I agree that is a potential problem. Big, ambitious projects require a lot of learning along the way, and you have no idea what hiccups you'll run into.

My suggested solution for this is two-fold: Make sure you include exploratory goals, and use more open-ended shorter term goals. For example, when I wrote my first book, I really fumbled my way through. I had the goal of writing a book, but I didn't set a timetable because I had no idea how long it would take (that turned out to be a mistake). I did set new intermediate and short-term goals as the project evolved; I learned how to make a YouTube channel, format text for printing, and I learned how to write that book.

Objectives & Key Results

OKR is a goal setting method used by Google that has gained popularity in the tech community. Both OKR and SMART were designed for businesses but have transitioned into personal use. OKR has yet to become as popular for personal goal setting as SMART, but that's probably because it is newer. There are two components to the OKR approach, *Objectives* and *Key Results*.

Objectives are single sentence statements that are more qualitative (feel based) than quantitative (numerically trackable). They are still time-bound; I recommend a semester. Objectives need to be motivational, daring, and have a significant impact on your life.

Key Results are action-oriented goals that are task oriented. Traditionally, you'll have three Key Results for every Objective, but you may have fewer or more (be careful with more). Key Results are a lot like semester goals.

Track OKR's weekly. You may want to rank your goals (also called goal stacking). You can only have one Priority 1 goal, but you could have multiple Priority 2 and 3 goals. A scoring system is often used, either grade based or score out of ten based. At Google, they use a system of 0 to 1. For example, if you're trying to get an A on your final presentation in public speaking and you get a B, you may score yourself 0.7 out of 1. That score may be higher or lower, depending on your assessment of how good you are at public speaking.

Pre-scoring goals can also be useful, it can remind you to put things in perspective once the period ends, which is particularly useful on more difficult KR's. It also can help with your planning going into a new semester. If you use this, resist the temptation to average your OKR grades into some personal GPA. Consider each OKR set separately.

One of the rules of OKR is that you can't change the KR's or the O until the end of the period (semester). That may work fine for you, but I think it's OK to change KR's if something is no longer attainable within a semester, rather than wait for the post-finals analysis. If you decide to do so, please give yourself a serious evaluation as to what went wrong. I don't think that changing Objectives within a semester is advisable. That's best done with a clear head during your break because of the overarching importance of Objectives.

If you're interested in the OKR framework, I recommend you check out the site eleganthack.com. The author, Christina Wodke, has some excellent articles on using OKR as a personal framework.

System Based

Essentially, systems are comprised of organizational skills and time management and lack traditional goal setting. In fact, it's pretty popular these days to eschew the practice of goal setting. Google "Systems not Goals" and you'll have dozens of blog articles to choose from.

The idea behind the system based approach is that you're likely to disappoint yourself by setting goals, because you won't hit the target every time. Critics warn that once you achieve a goal, you may end up in a "yo-yo" situation. For example, you get in shape by using the goal or running a marathon, you achieve that goal and run the marathon, but then you stop exercising.

It's further argued that goals make you unhappy in the short term by sending you the message that you aren't currently good enough. Further, system proponents allege that goals are unhealthy by distorting your understanding of what is in your control.

In my opinion, these criticisms can be addressed by a clear understanding of goals. Goals aren't goals if you hit them every time; there has to be a risk of failure. Goals that are intended to be lifelong, or very long duration will have subsidiary goals. For example, you may decide to run that marathon as a one-year goal that is part of a larger goal of living a healthy lifestyle.

I think that achieving or failing to achieve a goal allows you the opportunity to pivot and reconsider what you want to do. If the goal is a healthy lifestyle, there are plenty of other ways to get there. I don't believe that goals reduce your current happiness. Everyone has room for personal growth, as long as you remember that you won't be perfect at achieving your goals. **Goals should teach you; they should not dictate how you feel about yourself.**

I have one last issue with the systems approach. It completely ignores that you already have some goal in mind. If you study hard for a test, you have some goal in mind. If your in college, you have some goal in mind. Proper goal setting makes your motivation clearer and stronger while also preventing you from using negative goals.

When You Achieve Your Goal

Ironically, achieving your goals can land you in trouble. You deserve to take time out, relax, and celebrate. But, you can take it too far. Don Shula, the famous football coach, had a 24-hour rule. His players, coaches, and staff had 24-hours to celebrate a victory or mourn a defeat. After that, the chapter was closed, and it was time to prepare for the next week's game. Everyone is full of advice on how to get over defeat, but how do you get over victory?

I think you need to take a fixed amount of time to celebrate your achievement, and then you need to take a good look around. Even though you hit your goal, could you have done things better? If so, what were they? Look forward. Where are you now? Where do you want to go next? Where do you want to be? Set new goals and begin to pursue those.

Changing Goals

I'm not a big fan of changing or abandoning goals halfway through a semester, right after you bomb a test, or even right after you turn in your last final. Take some time after major events to compose yourself, put things in perspective, and evaluate your options. Don't change any significant goals in the middle of a semester. You don't want to make an emotionally charged decision. Don't mistake me, I'm not against changing goals at all. I just don't want you do to it for the wrong reasons.

Often, we change goals when we decide things are no longer attainable, or the goal is not worth enduring the pain it would take to get there. These can be a valid reasons for changing goals, but seriously look at your options before you give up. Check out the chapter on *Bad Test/Bad Class/Bad Semester* for more.

Here are some reasons people change goals and some considerations to keep in mind.

Fear – Are you afraid that things won't work out? Are you terrified that you'll never be accepted into medical school, or make it as a professional actor? There may be justifiable reasons for these concerns. It's tough, and I don't want to advise you one way or the other. In general, though, the way to achieving a goal is broader than you expect, and you can often come up with a way forward. If fear, and fear alone, is your reason for abandoning a goal that you truly have passion for, reconsider. Even if it turned out you were right (of course, you'd never know), you'd still deal with the regret of not knowing.

Happiness – Have you decided that you wouldn't be happy as a psychologist or accountant? It's a very valid reason to change a goal. I will say, though, there are a lot of different kinds of psychologists and accountants and that something interested you to those goals in the first place. Before you jump ship, consider what else achieving that goal may allow you to do.

Ability – Do you feel like you can't hack it in engineering or chemistry? Before you decide you can't do something, make sure you exhaust all of the resources at your disposal (check out the chapters on XXX). It's possible that engineering or dental school isn't for you, but if you talk to most engineers or dentists, they'll tell you that the road was hard at points.

New Information – You've found out that getting a Ph.D. isn't as sure a job track as you initially thought (that's true, by the way). You'll need to weigh your new information about the realities of a career, major, or lifestyle goal, with how passionate you are for the goal. People at the top of their profession generally do pretty well financially and have good job security.

Passion – If your heart isn't in it, your heart isn't in it. Make sure that you're not really afraid of failing, but only pursue goals that you're committed to.

Bad Goal Setting – Sometimes we bite off more than we can chew. We set goals that we're either loosely attached to (a lack of passion) or that don't fit well with our time in life and how we want to organize our life. If you feel like this is the case, try and determine why you set the goal to begin with. To go back to a fitness example, you may have decided to run a 10k to get in better shape, but there are many ways to accomplish the real goal of living a healthier life.

The Wrong Why – Look, no one wants to be broke forever, but for some of us money is more important than others. What's your motivation for wanting a giant house or a sports car? If you think that those things will make you happy, you're probably wrong. In fact, mortgaging your happiness for things is always a bad trade. That said, financial security and financial goals are important, but don't ever do something just for the money. Similarly, your "why's" should be internal. Don't do something because others will think highly of you or you'll "beat" your friends/enemies. It's a lousy way to go through life.

Remember that success takes innumerable forms and your definition will be unique to you. A life well lived is the life you want to live, where you feel that you have value, contribute, feel comfortable, and have quality relationships.

Time and Chance

I'm not a religious person, but I do love this quote from Ecclesiastes, "the race is not to the swift or the battle to the strong, nor food to the wise or wealth to the brilliant…. but time and chance happen to them all."

The role of chance in our lives is open for debate, but randomness certainly plays a large role in our life. From the moment of conception to who our parents are and what our childhood environment is like, we are being acted on by forces outside of our control, forces that often have no deliberate direction.

So, how do you account for the role of luck in life while setting goals and doing your best? To a large extent, that's a question you'll have to answer for yourself (assuming you are interested in such questions). I will, however, make some suggestions.

You can't do much about luck, good or bad. You can, however, put yourself in a position where good things are much more likely to happen and bad things are much less likely to happen. Your habits, goals, and all the related skills will expose you to the envelope of serendipity, and, in general, the harder you work the luckier you get.

Find some relief in the fact that there are things outside of your control. After all, if everything was in your control, you'd not only have terrible power but you'd also ultimately bear the consequences of every bad or good thing that happens to you. Bad things happen, good things happen, what matters isn't that they happen, it's how we react to them.

Finally, we tend to judge "bad luck" in the terms of the immediate results. It is bad luck to get rear ended, or to drop your notebook in a puddle, but who knows how that will ripple through your life. If that sounds a little cheesy, that's because it is. I don't think that makes it any less true. Life is a long game, play for time.

Resources

OKR Christina Wodke	eleganthack.com/the-art-of-the-okr/
Strides S.M.A.R.T Goal App	Apple & Android App Store
System Only James Clear	jamesclear.com/goals-systems

16 GET ORGANIZED

The Importance of Organization

A sound organizational system will save you time, stress, and improve your GPA. You'll get more done, and life will be easier. I can't stress organization enough. In my work with students as an academic coach and test prep tutor, **the differences between high achievers and middle of the road performers are organizational skills *and* the ability to prioritize.** (More on prioritization in the chapter on *Time Management*).

A good organizational system is simple, integrates into your life, and makes life easier.

How to Get Organized

Keep a Calendar
Keep a calendar. Seriously, keep a calendar! You'll have all your due dates, appointments, office hours, everything in your phone or on paper. I prefer calendar apps to physical calendars, because of the customizability and alerts. That said, if you're already organized and you love your paper planner, keep it. It's the backbone of getting and staying organized. The less things creep up on you, the less often you'll be in a frantic situation, and the easier it will be to move forward. Students who don't have some system of organization are always digging themselves out of trouble instead of moving forward.

| **Set Alerts &** | Set alerts. At first, you may even want to use them |
| **Look Ahead** | to tell you "15 minutes until Bio." Alerts for |

recurring daily items are nice, but to get the most out of alerts, think about the 'bigger ticket' items: exams, papers, group projects. Set notifications to tell you when items are due the next day, three days from now, one week, two weeks, etc. If you think it'll take you 7 days to get ready for that Bio midterm, set daily reminders starting at 9 days. **Use multiple alerts for every major project or test.**

Always give yourself a little extra room in case something awful (or awesome) happens. It'll keep your stress level from skyrocketing when the unexpected happens. Regularly check your calendar going two or three weeks ahead. You may realize that that you need less or more time to prepare for a test or complete a paper, but always err on the side of being notified a little too early.

Plan Ahead   Planning ahead goes hand-in-hand with alerts. It's critical that you understand that you'll be busier later in the semester. While alerts focus on specific tasks, planning ahead is more about structuring and positioning yourself to stay a half-step ahead of life.

Reset   This is the bigger version of planning ahead. Sit down and ask yourself questions about your organizational system. On a regular basis (put it in your calendar), ask yourself, what could make things easier and more efficient next week, next month, or next semester? What isn't working with my system?

This is the bigger version of planning ahead. Sit down and evaluate your organizational system. Ask yourself, what could make things easier and more efficient next month? What isn't working with my system?

Don't Lose Your Stuff

One Notebook Per Class – I'm a big fan of using a separate single subject notebook for each class. You'll automatically have all your lecture notes in one place, and it makes packing for the day simple. I suggest notebooks with a folder built-in and get a different color for every course. (Check out the resources for some great books/articles on this).

File & Take Pictures – The first thing you should do with your syllabus is take a picture of each page. The second thing you should do is put every important date in your calendar with appropriate notification times. The third thing you should do is file the syllabus away. You can put it in your notebook folder, but I recommend you keep a separate folder that stays at home.

Take pictures of any course materials, especially if they aren't online. Keep those photos on the cloud or on your device's memory, so that way you can always access what you need.

Use Binders for Printed Slides – If your professor puts lecture slides up, I suggest you print and use them for lecture notetaking (check out the chapter on Class & Notes). To keep these organized, get a three-ring binder and a hole punch.

Put Things in the Same Place – I'm not the neatest guy in the world (it takes effort for me), but my life is so much easier when I designate places for my physical belongings. This goes double for file management on my computers.

How to Stay Organized

1. **Use Your Calendar** – You can use your calendar to make you use your calendar. Sounds circular, right? Here's the trick: set your calendar to notify you every day to keep up with your calendar. In a semester or so, you'll get in the habit of checking your calendar every day. I suggest setting your reminder for at least half an hour after you wake up. Otherwise, you may begin to build up resentment towards your calendar (seriously).

2. **Start Strong** – The first day or two of class are devoted to the syllabus. Put all dates on the syllabus into your calendar, with details regarding the assignment, paper, or exam. If you combine these with alerts, you'll be forewarned and forearmed. This is incredibly helpful; the less assignments and assessments (quizzes and tests) sneak up on you, the easier it is to stay organized and stay prepared. You'll also save time by not having to login to your courses or find your paper syllabus.

3. **Use a To-Do List** – Use a prioritized to-do list or app to use pen and paper. Group things into *Must Do's*, *Should Do's*, and *Stretch Goals*. More on this in the *Time Management* chapter.

4. **Relationships Take Effort** – Your relationship with organization requires a little attention. Spend 10 – 15 minutes a day straightening up, putting things away, checking items on your to-do list, adding them to your calendar, etc. I've traditionally had a messy desk, but I find that I work better and am generally happier when it's clean.

5. **Think Strategically** – If you're disorganized, you'll have to train yourself to think about staying organized. When faced with a new task or new obligation, take a second and think about how it will change or "flow through" your organizational system.

Apps

There are dozens of organizational apps on the market (certainly more by the time you read this). Each app does a different job and has a different interface, and how well the app works for you depends—in my opinion—on how similar you and the app's designer(s) are.

You'll notice the advice I gave you in this chapter is concrete but requires customization by you. That's intentional because I feel a good organizational system is very personal.

I don't dislike apps, and in the *Time Management* chapter, I list an app that I use called Kanban Flow. But it can be tough to find an app that fits you. Here are some things I would consider:

All-in-one or specific job – You need to know what job the app is going to do. Don't hesitate to test drive a few, there may be features you want that you would have never thought of.

Meets you where you're at – If you're committing to a new organizational system (particularly if you're unorganized) you are already making major changes. The app needs to be simple and intuitive. If using the app feels like work, you're less likely to do it.

Simplicity – In general, the more powerful a piece of software, the more complex it is to use (ask anyone who has ever learned Photoshop). A complex app is fine, if that's what you want. What I mean by simplicity, is have clear roles for every component of your organizational system, and keep the number of parts limited. If you're using four or five apps to stay on top of things, you're not doing yourself any favors. I use two very simple apps for everything in my life from work to my daughter: Google calendar and Kanban Flow.

Resources

iProcrastinate Allows tasks to be broken down	Apple & Android App Store
Omni Focus Ios App	Omnigroup.com
Week Plan Time Blocking & Prioritization	weekplan.net

17 TIME MANAGEMENT & SELF-STARTING

We tend to view self-starting as spontaneous internal motivation. I think that's a bit silly. After all, we can't control how inspired we are. **Instead, focus on managing your time well and setting clear achievable goals, and you'll become a self-starter**. For the most part, people with an inability to self-start are suffering from uncertainty over where to start.

The Principals of Time Management

Vision   It's really difficult to establish good time management habits if you lose sight of *why* you're doing things in the first place. Time management takes motivation. You need to understand how time management will help you achieve your goals, and how each small task fits into a bigger scheme.

Prioritization Just like an emergency room taking the most critical patients first, you need to triage your tasks. Not all assignments and obligations are created equal, and while calling your grandmother is important, it's not as important as making flashcards for the anatomy practical next week.

One at a Time   Multitasking does not work. Brains just aren't built for multitasking when the tasks are meaningful. Multitasking drops IQ scores 15 points, one standard deviation, the same drop as if you'd stayed up all night or gotten drunk.

Be Reasonable Good time management practices require that you break big projects into component tasks and that you stay aware of your own limitations. If your goal is to study physics for five hours straight, you're likely going to falter. It's too long, and you'll end up distracted and unproductive. It's OK to take breaks, just don't set yourself to herculean efforts. You'll get frustrated with yourself, you won't see any progress, and you'll abandon time management.

Be Aware It's incredibly important to figure out how you work best. Play around with different times, change your surroundings, and try different methods of working and studying. Additionally, pay attention to what you do right before you work, and what you plan to-do right after. For example, I don't get a lot done in the afternoon if I have a big lunch. I get more done if I'm looking forward to doing something fun after I'm done working.

Time Management Strategies

Make your own combination of the list below. For example, I use numbers 1, 2, 3, 5, and occasionally 6 and 7.

1. **Use a Helpful To-Do List** – If you're doing this on paper, color-code or group tasks by importance. I use kanbanflow.com and have my list grouped as *To-Do, Do Today, Urgent, In Progress, & Done*. You can make a list like this on paper, but I prefer apps. Throughout the day, I re-sort my list, moving tasks into the In *Progress* and *Done* categories. You'll find some to-do apps in the resources section of this chapter.

2. **Break Big Projects Into Bite Sized Pieces** – Chunking projects is critical to managing yourself and making a to-do list useful. If you have a paper due in a week, don't put on the to-do list "paper." Instead, put "find and read three sources for paper." That's a discrete, achievable task. Doing this requires that you think about the steps involved in the project and make time estimates, which by itself is a huge benefit. Psychologically, putting "paper" down makes it incredibly intimidating to start. Find an accessible, achievable entry point so you can move that day's item from *Do Today* to *Done*.

3. **Frame the Day** – Start the day by updating your to-do list and setting or reinforcing your priorities. As you practice time management and acclimate to college, you'll get a better handle on both what is important and how long it will really take. My most productive days start by updating my to-do list. I feel more motivated, I set clear priorities, and I make better use of both block and scrap time.

4. **Do the Toughest Thing First *OR* Make Your Bed** – Once you've got your to-do list ready to go, it's time to get started on the day. There are two schools of thought: start your day by doing the toughest, most dreaded task or start your day by doing something simple that's entirely within your control (like making your bed).

   I do a bit of both, sometimes I need to get a really nasty task out of the way first because I'll be too anxious and preoccupied about it to focus on whatever else I need to do. Sometimes I need that little boost that comes from having gotten one thing out of the way, and I'll start by something simple like washing dishes or throwing in a load of laundry. The Resources section of this chapter has some great articles that will give you a more in-depth understanding of both approaches.

5. **Check-In** – Check-in on how you're using your time. It's incredibly easy to lose 10 or 20 minutes at a time. You need to take breaks (check item 6), but they need to be *intentional breaks*. No one is perfect at productivity, and it's tough when you get started. By checking in, you'll learn what to avoid during your productive time; everyone has their weaknesses (for me it's Wikipedia and Facebook).

6. **Pomodoros** – You can't focus forever, and you can't work your hardest for hours at a time. Trying to work without breaks is much less productive than attacking your work intensely and taking scheduled breaks. To maximize your productivity and vigor, I recommend the Italian time management technique called the Pomodoro. Here's how it works: work for 25 minutes and then take a five-minute break, go back to work for 25 minutes and then take another five-minute break. You do four 25-minute work periods and then take a fifteen-minute break. I've found that working that way has greatly improved both the quantity and quality of writing I produce.

Here's the trick: when you work, you don't do anything else. Your phone needs to be on airplane mode or silent, and you need to wait to get a drink or go to the bathroom until you have your break. Do whatever you want in your five-minute break but you *have to come back at the end*. That's the hardest part. To make it easier and more structured, use a timer. Kanbanflow.com has a great one, and it also comes as an app.

7. **Browser Blockers** – A browser blocker can make Pomodoros much easier. I use WasteNoTime, which allows me to block all websites for a set period. You can add sites to a "do not block" list, but be sensible. Keep your email, social media, etc. off of that list. While I use this with writing, it can be trickier to use for subjects like chemistry or math, where access to resources like YouTube can be invaluable.

8. **Block your Time** – This is sort of like a to-do list, except you create it in your calendar. For example, you may decide to go to the library and study biology after your 9 a.m. class until noon. Blocking works great for some, but there are a couple of potential pitfalls. Time sitting at the library, isn't the same thing as achieving measurable goals. You could sit at the library checking your phone every five minutes and learn very little about mitosis. The other problem is inflexibility. If you want to have lunch with a friend, instead of reading while eating, you will feel conflicted. If you opt to have lunch with your friend, your whole system is thrown off, and you'll need to plug back the activity you lost back into your calendar at a different time.

I think blocking works better when you leave open space, so you can shift blocks back and forth a half-an-hour or an hour. I've had students tell me that blocking worked great for them their first semester or two and then they moved away with it after they developed a routine and habits. If you're chronically unorganized and overwhelmed, partial blocking may provide the training wheels you need to become a lean, mean, high GPA machine. Blocking works best (in my opinion) with a separate to-do list.

9. **Use the Scrap Time** – Life is full of 15-minute blocks where you're waiting at for class to start, public transport, etc. Try and use these effectively. If nothing else, take a look at your calendar and update your to-do list.

10. **Learn to Say No** – You'll find (or have found) this advice repeated in the *Get Involved* chapter. One of the most important personal skills you can develop is the ability to say, "sorry I can't." I don't just mean when your friends want to go out, but also when you're invited to join a formal activity or take a leadership role. If it's not in your heart or you feel it will stretch you too thin, politely decline. You won't be helping anyone, especially yourself if you can't do a solid job.

    Saying no is a tough skill to learn at first, and you may never master it completely, but do try. You'll eventually feel relieved when you say no to something you didn't want to do or didn't have the time for.

11. **Time Management Takes Time** – It takes time to learn how to manage your time, and you have to put time into using your time effectively. I promise you, learning to manage your time will vastly increase your performance and your opportunities down the line. And the time you spend on time management is more than paid back by the time you save.

Dealing with Backlog

Many of you may be coming to time management already drowning in a backlog of tasks caused by poor time management. The first step is to prioritize your tasks. When you prioritize, your goal is to keep from falling farther behind. Sort things into three categories, *Now*, *Later*, and *Never*. By Never, I mean that it won't have any significant ramifications on your life if the task ever gets done. Don't be afraid to throw things into the Never category, you can still complete the tasks if you choose.

After you've triaged your task list, focus on the *Now* items that will keep you from falling farther behind. Sometimes that means upcoming due dates are more important than past due dates.

Becoming a Self-Starter

When you're looking for your first real job after college you'll find almost every job description includes "self-starter" or it's analogues "self directed", "ambitious", or "go-getter". It's easy to disregard self-starting as a buzzword or—even worse—think of it as a fixed quantity (you either got it or you don't). **Just like intelligence, talent, organizational skills, or anything else I discuss in this book, being a self-starter is about consciously deciding to** *be* **a self-starter and making decisions accordingly.**

Research backs this up, self-starters are those who have a high degree of "internal locus of control". As mentioned in the meta-chapter at the beginning of this section, an internal locus of control is the belief that you have a strong impact on your life, and the outcomes that happen in your life. The belief that you are, to a large extent, the master of your own destiny is very important for your well being.

Here's the wrinkle: making independent decisions gives you a feeling of control, which makes you feel more independent. So, the more independent decisions you make, the stronger your internal locus of control. But, if you're not making a lot of your own choices now—deferring to others or letting circumstances dictate your behavior—how do you get in the habit of making your decisions and feeling ownership over your life?

Start small. You don't have to make huge decisions initially, but start by expressing preferences or choosing things where normally you would take what was offered or having someone else choose. Pick a spot for dinner instead of having your friend choose. Tell your group which part of the presentation you want to do, instead of taking what no one else wants.

Start somewhere. Once you get the knack of making decisions for yourself (you may already be there), the real test is getting off your butt to get started on that paper you're dreading or whatever other nightmare life has in store for you. Just find a place to start, break down large projects into bite sized pieces. Start somewhere easy, to give yourself early success and the feeling of ownership. Even completing 1% of a project will show you that 1) the project can be finished and 2) you can do it.

Start now. The enemy of self-starting is the base level anxiety that comes with putting things off. I think we often confuse this anxiety with fear of the task itself, wrapping the task up and making it far scarier than it needs to be. Sitting down to start doesn't mean you have to finish. But do yourself a favor and get started.

Resources

Kanban To Do List & Pomodoro Timer	Kanbanflow.com Apple & Android App Store
Eat the Frog	theartofsimple.net/start-your-day-by-eating-a-frog/
Make Your Bed Adm. William H. McRaven (his book is also excellent)	nytimes.com/2017/09/02/style/how-to-make-your-bed.html
Backlog vs. To-Do	agilesparks.com/blog/backlog-vs-to-do/
Epic Win Time Management App with a RPG component	Apple & Android App Store
Week Plan Time Blocking & Prioritization	weekplan.net

19 BUILD YOUR ACADEMIC LIFE

The chief difference between high school and college is structure. In high school, structure is provided. It's also enforced, largely through disciplinary action taken by your parents/guardians or by the school. In college, you provide your own structure. The previous section of the book dealt with the skills you need to create your own structure. Now I want to turn your attention to how to respond to the lack of structure (handholding) in the classroom.

Academic success is built day-by-day. It's built by paying attention in class, taking notes, giving yourself ample time to prepare for tests and to complete assignments, and building good professional relationships with your professors and your advisor. That's it.

Coping with a Lack of Academic Structure
One of the hardest transitions for many students is the open-ended nature of papers and tests. You know you have a test on Chapters 4 – 8, but that's all. You know you need 10 pages on James Buchanan, but that's about all you're given. No one is checking in on you.

Professors respond to questions, but they typically don't initiate. They will answer your questions, they will spend time with you discussing assignments and exams, but they aren't going to anticipate your questions. So, if you're one of the many students who find the lack of structure discomfiting, use your professor. If you don't want to ask in front of the class, ask before/after class or during office hours. In time you'll better understand the expectations of college and you'll be more comfortable with the lack of structure.

Freedom Costs Responsibility
Responsibility and freedom is almost a 1 for 1 trade. In my life, I found I had more freedom in college than high school, but I had more responsibility. I had more freedom as an employee than I did in college, but I had added responsibilities. I have more freedom now that I'm self-

employed, but I have a great deal of responsibility, because I'm not guaranteed a salary, there are no sick days, and no one actually makes me do anything. One thing I've learned: **if you don't work hard enough to meet your responsibilities, you lose your freedom.**

You've taken on significant responsibility in all aspects of life, including your academics. You have a lot of freedom over what you study, when you take classes, when you do your coursework, and even if you attend class. How you handle that freedom, and how you meet those responsibilities will, more than anything else, determine where you are in four years.

Change Your Relationship with Optional

In high school optional meant, "sweet, I don't have to do it." I encourage you to change how you feel about optional. In college and in the professional world, it's the "optional" stuff that sets you apart. **Taking on the optional is the path to success.** Tutoring, office hours, visiting speakers, etc. are optional activities that help you develop as a student and a person. It's not about any extra-credit you may receive, it's about establishing a habit of taking advantage of opportunities, exploring new ideas, and putting in the extra effort. I'd like your relationship with the optional to be, "I'll do it unless I can't."

Plan

This is what happens to all too many students: the semester starts off super easy and nothing really happens or is due for a few weeks. Even if you mess up a couple little quizzes or assignments, you'll more than make up for it when the bigger ticket stuff comes along. So what if you're a little behind in chem or math, you'll just catch up before that first exam.

The first exams come along and you're way behind. You squeak out a B, a C, and a few D's and F's. Now you're behind the 8-ball. That's ok, you won't make that mistake again, because you're just dropping the tough courses (hey, take them next time), and that will give you more time on the other classes. But, the next set of exams comes around and your grades are the same....

Here's what went wrong: You spent your time reacting instead of being proactive. The semester starts easy, so you react to that and establish a pattern for yourself that's tough to shake.

Here's how to fix it: On the first day of class, you get a syllabus. Most students take a quick look at the syllabus, see how the grading works, when the tests/major assignments are, and what the attendance policy is. Do that.

But your syllabus is also a roadmap to your success in the course.

Pay attention to the topics; try to anticipate anything that may be difficult for you. Put all your dates in your calendar (see the chapter on *Organization*). Look for any tips on what successful students do in the course, and if they aren't on the syllabus, the professor will mention them in class. If successful students use on-campus tutoring, make it a point to locate and visit that tutor in the first week. Set a good pattern for yourself. Start studying now. **You have two choices at the beginning of the semester, you can build a lead on your courses for when things get tough, or you can borrow against the future and make your life stressful and your grades suffer.**

When it Comes to Work: Smart > Hard

Hard work is necessary and I believe it's a reward unto itself. But there's no honor in making work harder than it needs to be. Consider a man showing you his in-ground pool. Would you be impressed if he told you he dug it by hand with a pick and shovel?

I wouldn't. Frankly, I'd think he was an idiot. Not only is it a huge waste of time to dig it by hand, there's no way the work would be done nearly as well as a professional excavator could do it.

Working hard isn't a goal, it's a means to achieving goals. Always ask, what is the most efficient way to get to my objective? If it's a good grade on a test, staring at the same textbook and notes for hours is like digging a pool with a shovel. You'll spend a ton more time and it won't work out quite as well. The same applies to any major assignment in college. Always have a plan, always be organized, and always prioritize.

In This Section

Go to Class & Take Notes – You need to show up, but what you do when you're there can make your life much easier.

Learn to Learn: How to Study – Time studying is not the same as progress. I discuss several methods for studying and how you should mix and match them depending on your preferences and your courses.

Ace Tests & Assignments – You have a goal, make a plan. I discuss several assessment types and give you some pointers for making life easy.

Deal with Professors – You have to manage your relationships with professors like an adult; I give you some guidelines and insight into their point of view.

20 GO TO CLASS & TAKE NOTES

A career army officer once told me that 95% of success in the military came down to, "right time, right place, right uniform." I think that's true of all workplaces, including your collegiate classroom.

In-Class Strategies

Show Up – You have to show up to class, even if it's not required. But just showing up isn't sufficient; you need to be prepared and ready to learn. If you're staying ahead on your courses, you'll get much more out of the lecture because you'll have done the reading or looked at the practice problems beforehand. If you're behind, you're much less likely to keep falling behind (check out the *Time Management* chapter on how to deal with backlog).

Participate – Ask and answer questions. If speaking up is difficult for you, set a weekly goal of participating in each class at least once. Talk to your professor before or after class whenever you have a question that may require a lengthy answer, or is somewhat off-topic.

Take Good Notes – Quality notes have a few key characteristics no matter what course you're taking or note taking system you're using. And yes, I do think you should use a system, either one of the ones I introduce on the next few pages or one you develop.

- ✓ Good notes are simple. Use keywords and don't worry about writing in complete sentences.
- ✓ Good notes are usable. Taking notes is helpful, but you're only getting part of the benefit if you can't read your notes or decipher their meaning.

✓ Good notes are distilled. Only write down what matters. Sometimes this can be tricky to figure out until you get to know your professor better.
✓ Good notes are an outline of the lecture.

PowerPoint Notes – If your professor uses PowerPoint (or other slide software), your job is to fill in the gaps between slides and take down any details that are emphasized more in the lecture than they are on the slides. How you do this is up to you. You can print out the slides in handout form, or you can take notes in a notebook, on a laptop or pad, and when you review the notes combine them with the slides. If you're using PowerPoint slides/guided notes provided by your professor, it's crucial to summarize the slide content in your own words when you review your notes.

Review, Review – Review the same day, or at the latest, the next day. The longer you wait, the less you'll retain. How you review your notes depends on your preferences, how you learn, and the course. Don't be afraid to switch strategies from course to course. Regardless of what you choose to do, the key is to engage with the material and think critically about it. Here are some methods for reviewing notes:

✓ Transcribe and expound on your notes. Turn your concise notes into more full fleshed summaries that are organized like an outline.
✓ Connect it to the end-of-chapter questions. Use your textbook to answer the end-of-chapter questions based on your notes.
✓ Fill-in omitted or additional details within your notebook.
✓ Create flashcards based on your notes.
✓ Create summaries, questions, and keywords based on the Cornell Method (see the next page).

You can use one or all of these simultaneously. Be careful not to slip into rote recopying of your notes; you need to *think* about what you're doing and how it fits in the larger context of the course. Periodically (weekly or every two weeks), go back through all of your transcribed notes for the entire course.

Note Taking Approaches

Cornell Method – You create two columns, the left is 1/3rd of the width of the page or even a little less. Take your general notes in the bigger column. The left column is for topics/keywords. Leave 6 – 7 lines blank at the bottom of the page. Within 24 hours of class, review your notes and write summaries/questions at the bottom of each page.

Disadvantage – This wouldn't work particularly well for me because I'm a sloppy writer. I'm far more comfortable with transcribing my notes later and organizing them while transcribing. You can use the Cornell method as a way of organizing notes when you transcribe them.

Split-Page Method – The Split-Page Method is very similar to the Cornell Method. You'll create two columns, the right for lecture notes and the left for an outline of the corresponding part of the textbook. Alternatively, you can use three columns: the middle for lecture notes, the right for a textbook outline, and the left for keywords and topics.

Disadvantage – The Split-Page Method has the same problem as the Cornell Method. Depending on how you write, you can end up with a big, unhelpful mess.

Mind Maps – Are flow charts you create instead of regular (linear) notes. Mind maps are great at organizing the relationships between concepts. Proponents argue that regular note-taking can be boring, exhausting, and inefficient. For some of you, mind maps will work great. In the Resources section of this chapter, you'll find a free app for creating mind maps.

Disadvantage – Mind maps are tough to implement if you have no idea what direction the lecture will be going (being ahead in the course is more important if you plan to use mind maps). You also may have trouble organizing them spatially because of page size.

Flow Based – Flow based note taking is the brainchild of Scott H. Young, who has published some excellent books on academic success and writes a terrific blog (check out the Resources section of this chapter). The idea is somewhat similar to the mind map technique, in that you'll use arrows and diagrams to create conceptually organized notes. It can be a great note taking strategy if you're doing a good job staying ahead in the course and you're willing to go through a significant learning curve.

Disadvantage – I think flow based note-taking has the same problem as mind maps: it can be tough to implement if you're walking in to the lecture unprepared. Like mind maps, I think flow based note taking is a great review strategy.

Technology & Note Taking

I'm not a huge fan of laptop notes. You're somewhat restricted by the format, and you don't retain the material as well. Typing notes encourages an almost verbatim transcription of the lecture, which is fine for facts, but it hampers conceptual learning. I encourage you to take notes by hand, or on a tablet using a stylus. Recent research has shown that handwriting notes is more effective than typing them.

Note-Taking Strategies

Note-taking is a skill, and, like any skill, it has to be developed. If you have the right intention and are conscientious about note taking, you'll develop your own style. Below are some suggestions that are applicable to everyone, regardless of your note taking approach, format, or course material. Remember the purpose of note taking is to be able to use your notes later.

Use Abbreviations – If you're writing "punctuated equilibrium" for your evolutionary bio class 20 times per lecture, you may want to shorten it to PE.

Pick and Choose – Be selective about what you write down. Often, less is more as you'll be able to pull out the main ideas and most relevant details from your notes at a later point.

More Paper Not Less – Don't crowd your paper to the point it's confusing or illegible. The more you space out your notes (within reason) the easier it is to understand the key points later.

Use Your Own Words – Paraphrase main ideas in your own words. It will help your understanding, retention, and your notes will be easier to decipher later.

Mark Potential Test Questions – If your professor says it'll be on the test, mark it in your notes. If your professor seems particularly interested in a topic or fact, or they says its very important, mark it.

Resources

The Cornell Method	lsc.cornell.edu/notes.html
Mind Maps Discussion & App	Mindmeister.com/blog/effective-note-taking/
Flow Based Scott H. Young	scotthyoung.com/blog/2008/03/06/learn-more-study-less-flow-based-notetaking/
Technology & Note Taking Susan Dynarski	gse.harvard.edu/news/uk/17/08/note-taking-low-tech-often-best

21 LEARN TO LEARN: HOW TO STUDY

Six Study Principles

There are as many different styles of learning as there are learners. While I think the principles below apply to everyone, you'll want to customize their application to fit you. **The most useful thing you can learn is how you learn best.**

1. **Eat the Frog**. In the *Time Management* chapter, I write about two ways to start the productive part of your day, "making the bed" and "eating the frog." When it comes to studying, I strongly suggest eating the frog. Start studying with the meanest, nastiest, subject then move on to easier work. By tackling the tough stuff when you're fresh, you'll learn more and feel less frustrated. You also won't be dreading your tough course(s) when you're working on your other courses.

2. **Ask for Help.** Your college has a ton of resources available, but you have to take the initiative. You can ask for help from your professor or TA, at math/writing labs, from free campus tutoring, or from your classmates and other peers. Take advantage. **Ask for help before your situation becomes an emergency.** To analogize, you need someone to teach you how to swim, not save you from drowning.

   How do I know I need help? If you're following a solid organizational system and time management structure, you'll know earlier, because you have fewer excuses for confusion and poor grades. Symptoms of needing help are the feeling of falling farther behind, frustration that "shuts you down," inability to follow the lecture, and, of course, bad grades.

3. **Sleep & Stay Healthy.** Chronic sleep deprivation takes about 15 points off of your IQ. Don't worry; you'll get it back once you start living a reasonable lifestyle. You also need to get some exercise (walking counts), take breaks, eat well, and feel good about yourself. Check out the chapters on *Eating, Sleeping, & Exercising* and *Mental Health* for actionable advice.

4. **Stay Flexible & Always Evaluate.** There are a ton of ways to study. Reading, Practice Problems (learn to love 'em), YouTube, Quizlet, reviewing/transcribing notes, office hours, tutoring, etc. Play around somewhat with what methods work best for each of your classes. Vary your methods, what works best for one course, may not be best for another, even if both courses are in the same discipline. In the next section of this chapter, I go over a toolkit of learning methods, pick and choose among them. **Note: you need to use multiple tools to learn most effectively.**

   You may be familiar with the (overly used) categories of visual learners, auditory learners, and kinesthetic learners. These classifications can be helpful, but people don't just learn "one way". Play around with what works for you, and don't feel beholden to any classification.

5. **Environment Matters –** Environment isn't just where you study, it's what you surround yourself with, what tools you use, what you wear, and what you listen to. I recommend that you make a habit of going to the library—check out the chapter on *Habit Formation* for more. If you choose to study in your dorm/apartment/home, shut the door. You may not want to walk to the library or think it's wasting time, but if you're routinely distracted the library is the best option. The best study spots have ample natural light, are quiet, and are comfortable (but not too comfortable). I also recommend you check out Cal Newport's Adventure Studying; you'll find his article in this chapter's resources.

   I had a friend in college who said, "finals week at the library is like prom: dress to impress." It made him feel more confident and decisive—great attitudes for studying.

I think there is something about intentionality, and I like the idea of "getting ready" to study. If you want to study in your pajamas, take a shower or brush your teeth before studying. It will serve as a signal that you're getting ready to work, not just hang out or nap. You'll also have fewer excuses to get up and do something else.

As far as headphones go, I suggest that you swap out your playlist for classical music or ambient noise. Lyrics tend to be distracting. If you don't like traditional classical music, check out instrumental movie soundtracks or a modern composer like Philip Glass. You can also use nature sounds, waves, or white noise apps. Set your phone on Do Not Disturb or airplane mode.

6. **Set a Schedule & Create Habits.** Consider chunking out library time on your calendar. I recommend that you go to the library (or good study place) almost every day and, insomuch as possible, at the same time and for the same duration. You'll train your brain to work at those times, and you'll soon develop a wonderful habit. Stick with it; it can be hard at first. Check out the chapter on *Habit Formation* for more.

Your Toolkit

At the end of the day, the purpose of going to class and taking notes is to learn and then apply what you learn. Significant research has been done on learning approaches, where they work, how they are best used, and how much help they provide.

Learning Strategies that Work

Distributed Practice is the opposite of cramming. Distributed practice requires you to revisit the material periodically. In my opinion, you should aim for working on each course almost every day.

When it Works: Distributed practice works very well over a broad range of disciplines and course structures.

How to use it: set aside one or two Pomodoros (check the chapter on *Time Management*) for each class (25 – 50 minutes). Review your notes, engage in the active summary method I introduce later, create mind maps, etc. Remember, the more active you are the better off you'll be.

What to Avoid: Time on task is not the same as actual productivity. Passively rereading your notes will do little to nothing for your grades. The key, as always, is to be active and engaged.

Drawbacks: American textbooks are topically organized and don't spent time on in-text review (like practice problems or summaries from earlier in the book). For classes with cumulative skills, topical organization is not usually as much of an issue because the skills you use in a problem set encompass your entire semester (more or less). I do, however, recommend that you regularly revisit material from earlier in the semester, reworking problems and reviewing material.

Practice Tests are amazing. If your professor provides them great. If they don't create your own using your textbook, in-class review notes, and quiz questions (more on this later).

When it Works: I think practice tests are invaluable for all disciplines.

How to Use it: Not all practice tests are created equal. Practice tests that require you to engage in open-ended problem solving or recall are much better preparation tools. Even if your final will be multiple choice, you'll benefit from making an essay, or short answer, practice test to work with. More practice tests are better. You can beat a single practice test to death, diminishing the return on your time to almost nothing. For more on how to write your own practice test, look later in the chapter.

You may also find old exams available through your student organization (particularly fraternities/sororities) or available for purchase at shops near campus. In general, using old exams doesn't violate the honor code at colleges, but you may want to check to make sure.

What to Avoid: Don't stare at the same practice test over and over, it loses it's value. Also, work the practice test before using the answers or comparing answers with someone else. Don't pile up practice test after practice test, space them out in the days leading up to an exam.

Drawbacks: You've got to be careful with your answers, particularly if you don't have an answer key for a provided practice test or if you create your own.

Elaborative Interrogation involves asking "why" questions. You are elaborating on the material and trying to make connections. I always think of this as focusing on "why things work." It may remind you a bit of small children, who often ask a series of why based questions, "why is the sky blue?"

When it Works: Elaborative interrogation works for a broad array of disciplines (even math), particularly those where there is a causal connection that can be used to underpin what would otherwise be memorization. It may not work very well if you're terrible at a subject or you don't have much of a background in it. In short, it works really well with lists of connected facts.

How to Use It: Instead of memorizing a list of facts, **ask yourself why things happen; elaborative interrogation is about understanding the relationship between facts/ideas**. So long as you are asking the right questions (the answers should be findable in lecture notes or the relevant textbook sections), you're probably on the right track. If you're having trouble getting started, the end of chapter questions in your text can be a good starting point. Using the example above, you may ask yourself, "why is the sky blue?" You'd answer, "because the atmosphere scatters more blue light than red light." Then you'd ask "why does the atmosphere scatter more blue light than red light?" and answer, "because of light's interaction with oxygen and nitrogen molecules."

What to Avoid: Don't get too off-topic. Remember, you want to stay focused on what's important. Also, be careful that you're answering correctly.

Drawbacks: There's some indication that elaborative interrogation doesn't work well with very complex material or items that are not fact based.

Self-Explanation is pretty well named. It's where you explain concepts, material, or the process of solving a problem to yourself as though you were teaching.

When it Works: Self-explanation is effective for most disciplines.

How to Use it: It's the old adage, "the best way to learn something is to teach it." In this case, you'll be teaching it to yourself. I do think, however, that this is a wonderful strategy for study groups, particularly when combined with practice tests.

What to Avoid: Be careful that you don't teach yourself bad information, and make sure you have a good grasp on what's actually important—otherwise you may spend a bunch of time on relatively trivial topics.

Drawbacks: Self-explanation can be time intensive, but I think it's usually worth the effort.

Interleaved Practice runs opposite the standard study model. Instead of "blocking" time to study a single concept, you'll mix (interleave) various topics. Interleaved practice has been shown to be very effective on math, as it helps students better classify and categorize problems. It has the added benefit of a built-in review.

When it Works: Interleaving has been studied in math, but I think it works well with any concept heavy course.

How to Use It: Set aside some time to review the previous unit whenever you study. Periodically—at least once a week—pick a section from farther back in the semester and work through it's material and problems as well.

What to Avoid: Be careful that you don't spend too much time "reviewing" material that you know as an excuse for not mastering the most recent topics.

Drawbacks: There's not a ton of research on when interleaving works and why it works. That said, it's my feeling that interleaving probably works best in courses where learning and skills are cumulative.

Learning Strategies that Work Differently Than You'd Think

Summarization by itself is not very productive. It can be, however, if you really know what you're up to (check later in the chapter). Summarization is, essentially a "family of strategies" and is incredibly dependent on the quality of your summaries.

When it Works: I think summarizing works best in concept heavy courses that aren't problem based. Again, though, the quality of your summary is paramount.

How to Use It: Good summaries are written in your own words, brief, and visually cluster ideas together. Engagement is key. Use alongside other strategies like self-explanation, or elaborative interrogation.

What to Avoid: Don't copy the text or your notes by rote. It's a waste of time.

Highlighting/Underlining key text is a low yield strategy for many students as they don't use it properly. Most students either highlight too much, highlight too little, or highlight the wrong things. Studies have shown that students do better on test questions that correspond with highlighted text, and a little worse on test questions where the answer had not been highlighted during reading.

When it Works: Highlighting works best in conjunction with other strategies, particularly when the material is main idea driven.

How to Use it: Don't highlight on the fly. The more you think about the text, the more you'll absorb and the better your highlights will be. I like reading a paragraph and then going back and highlighting. You don't have to do that, necessarily, but it's very important that you be deliberate about what you're highlighting and why.

What to Avoid: A commonly accepted reason for why highlighting should work is that it separates text out, indicating that it is important. Highlight too much and the text is no longer separate. Highlight too little and you miss too much information. I think there is a personal element here; your ideal highlighting will be unique to your learning style. That said, if you've only got four words on a page highlighted, or four words not highlighted, you're probably doing it wrong.

Mnemonics/Acrostics use associations with words, concepts, or images that you're already comfortable with. For example, if you wanted to remember that *blanca* is the Spanish word for *white*, you may associate *blanca* with the image of a white piece of copy paper. Acrostics are rhymes, sentences, or phrases where the first letter of each word represents a fact that belongs in some order. Please Excuse My Dear Aunt Sally is often used to represent the order of operations in arithmetic: Parenthesis, Exponents, Multiplication, Division, Addition, Subtraction. Mnemonics are very helpful, in general, for foreign languages, esoteric vocabulary, names, and technical terms. Acrostics are useful for memorize processes or parts that have an order (Med students love 'em).

The use of acrostics and mnemonics is limited by how close the association is and how much sense it makes to you. There is also evidence that the use of mnemonics can be harmful to long term retention.

When it Works: I like mnemonics for remembering processes, protocols, and language.

How to Use it: Mnemonics and acrostics really only work if you don't have to "reach" too far to make up or remember the association. The association needs to be clear and obvious to you. So you may want to adapt existing ones to something you like better. Mnemonics and acrostics should be used with other techniques, like elaborative interrogation.

What to Avoid: If a mnemonic doesn't make sense to you, then alter it or disregard it altogether. If you're really stretching to come up with a mnemonic, it's probably not going to be very helpful.

Imagery for Text Learning involves picturing what is happening in the text. Imagery for text learning is more broadly applicable than mnemonics.

When it Works: Surprise, surprise, imagery works best when the text/concepts are easily pictured. It is particularly effective for processes and spatially related items.

How to Use it: It's important that the images you form are clear and clean. You need to have a good notion of what it "should" look like—hence you need to have, or be developing, some mastery already. I recommend you use it in conjunction with other strategies like summarization, self-explanation, and/or elaborative interrogation.

What to Avoid: Don't stretch too far to come up with your images. If you use a YouTube video (or something similar) to better understand what your image(s) should look like, make sure that you create your own image *without* looking at the reference material. Again, imagery works best when the material is easily imagined.

Rereading is one of the most used strategies. It's also one of the least effective. It's not so much that rereading is bad as it's just not as good as other, more active strategies.

When it Works: Rereading works for most subjects and is effective regardless of the length of the text. When rereading works, it's probably because your brain rereads differently than it reads. I would use rereading in courses where the professor relies heavily on the textbook(s) and/or the exams are created by the textbook authors.

How to Use It: Most of the benefit of rereading comes from the second reading (the first reread). Additionally, you should lag your second reading by a day or a few days to get the most retention. If you decide to reread, do so in conjunction with one or more other strategies.

What to Avoid: Don't reread passively, It's very easy for rereading to become nothing more than eyes moving across the page, so keep checking in with yourself to make sure you're active. Engage the text, look to take away something different on your second time through. Don't lean too heavily on rereading, you're usually better off summarizing your lecture notes while pulling additional details or enhancing your perspective with the text.

Ok, I Read All of That, but What Do I Do?

It depends on you, your learning style, your courses, and your professors. Always employ multiple approaches, and **the more active the better**. I think working and creating your own practice tests is incredibly helpful. I also think summaries can be incredibly useful, *but only when combined with other strategies.*

Writing a Good Summary

I think summaries can be the "backbone" strategy for a lot of classes. Start by re-writing your lecture notes in different words while looking at the textbook. Augment your notes with information and explanations from the textbook, **but always use your own words**. While summarizing, engage in self-explanation, and also try in elaborative interrogation, text base imagery, make mnemonics, etc. when appropriate. You can write your summary out in sentence form, in mind map form (check the previous chapter), or using the Cornell Method. Use multiple strategies and be as active as possible. Ultimately, you know the difference between thinking hard and being passive. If you aren't thinking, you aren't getting much return on your time and effort.

Writing Your Own Practice Tests

Practice tests should be the core of your test prep approach. If you don't have access to a professor's tests, or even if you do, I strongly suggest you take a shot at writing your own once you've worked through what's provided. Here's how to get started making your own practice tests:

1. **Know the Format** – Will the test be multiple choice, short answer, essay, or problem based? **In general, it's best to "overprepare." So, if the exam will be multiple choice, make your practice test short answer. If it's short answer, make your practice test an essay exam.**

2. **Use Your Notes** – Mark your notes up with potential questions. If you're especially clever (or paid attention to the last chapter), you'll have done this while taking your notes.

3. **Use Slides/Course Materials** – If your professor uses powerpoint slides or provides other course materials, use them to create questions.

4. **Use Your Textbook** – The beginning/end of chapter objectives are a great source for potential questions.

5. **Use Your Assignments** – Math/Science courses that are heavy on assignments provide a built-in question bank for you to work on. Particularly if your course uses a resource like MyMathLab, MyChemLab, or Aleks.

6. **Make it Realistic** – Initially focus on making sure you cover all the important material. Later, write new questions or divide up the questions to approximate the length of the test (this is particularly important if you have trouble finishing tests or test anxiety). When you aren't sure, give partial answers. In essence, take it like a real test.

7. **Ask Your Professor** – Show your professor the practice test you made and ask if you're hitting the important points. Seriously, do this. They will help point out where you're off, and they'll likely be impressed with your efforts.

8. **Make Sure You're Right** – Practice tests lose their effectiveness if you don't answer the questions correctly. Make sure you're right. I recommend sharing the tests you write class and working through them with classmates.

Assigned Reading

That huge stack of books from the bookstore (hopefully from Amazon, it's *way* cheaper to rent books) is intimidating. There's good news and bad news. The good news is that you won't really have to read all of that. Most courses—particularly intro courses—don't use the whole text or spread it out over two semesters. The bad news is there's still a ton of reading.

You'll also find that different professors use text books in very different ways. For many professors, the textbook is little more than supplemental material, while others rely more heavily on the book and its resources. You're more likely to have actually "read" any smaller books that go along with your courses.

Assigned Reading – Your textbook is not a novel, and you don't have to start at the beginning. Start by reading the end of chapter summary and questions, and use that information to figure out what you *need to learn*. Use the end of chapter questions to break the material into smaller, easily digestible portions. Taking breaks (using the Pomodoro or another method) is also beneficial.

Improving Reading Comp – Textbooks are laid out to draw your attention to what is important. Pay attention to bolded and italicized terms, as well as any colored callouts or blocked text. If you're working on a subject that has example problems throughout the chapter, work those examples step-by-step.

If you're having trouble keeping your focus while reading, interact with the text. The more you engage with the text, the more you'll retain and the less tedious it will feel. Here are some methods for interacting with assigned reading. I recommend using at least two.

   ✓ Use a highlighter or, at a minimum, a pen to mark up the text. Take notes in the margins. Remember, highlighting only works if you highlight the *right amount* of text and you're paying attention when you do it.

- ✓ Add notes from the reading to relevant parts of your course notes If you plan on doing this, take your class notes on only the front side of each notebook page or use the split page/Cornell method.
- ✓ Read-out-loud to yourself or mouth the words. This will slow down your reading speed, provide an auditory input, and improve your retention.
- ✓ Pause and paraphrase what you've just read, either as a summary or as an answer to one of the end of chapter questions.

Math/Quantitative Strategies

Reading Math Books – Frankly, math books can be really hard to read. Treat your math reading like it's guided math homework. Do the example problems, step-by-step. You may need to do them multiple times. Find the differences between questions. Follow each problem line-by-line. What makes the problem solving process change? For some people, working from the solution backwards to the problem is beneficial, give it a shot.

Be careful about ignoring examples that seem to be repetitive; it's likely that the author is trying to illustrate a subtle change.

The same approach works for economics, accounting, chemistry, physics, etc. The textbook writers are geared towards using the shortest and, to them, the simplest explanations, but, often that isn't very helpful to those who are not math inclined. Do your best and take your time, focus on the practice problems and examples throughout the chapter. If you find your textbook absolutely unintelligible, work through a bit, find a good YouTube video, and go back to see if the text makes more sense.

Summary Sheets – Jot down formulas, definitions, relationships, and concepts. Include a practice problem or two and annotate each step. It doesn't have to be one page; you can have multiple. Be careful with going on too long; there's a tradeoff between completeness and usability. Summary sheets will force you to think about the material in a new way and prioritize, and they're a huge help on homework problems.

Practice – Above all, you have to practice. Find additional practice problems online, if necessary. If you're using Pearson's Mymathlab.com as part of your course (which is very common), then I recommend that you rework all of your practice problems as a start, or major component of, your exam review strategy.

Use Resources – Ask questions before or after class, go to office hours for your professor or TA, and use your school's free tutoring. Many institutions have dedicated facilities with tutors available as a first come first serve basis. Start early! Even if you're doing fine, occasional tutoring is incredibly helpful, and it'll make your life easier. I recommend that you see a tutor at least once for every quantitative course you take.

Math Anxiety – Is a very real thing. In my work as a test-prep tutor, I address it on a daily basis. If you can overcome your math anxiety, not only will you be happier and perform better, but you'll have more major and career options. I hate to hear that someone threw options out the window because the major required a little bit of math.

Math anxiety causes poor performance; poor performance causes math anxiety. You end up in a feedback look, and you'll need to work hard on getting over your math anxiety to break that cycle.

Find Help

Your grades are your grades but don't go it alone. I strongly recommend you avail yourself of the tutoring, writing labs, office hours, and TA access that your college affords you. Additionally, I suggest you start or join study groups for all of your courses. Students in study groups get better grades: you'll fill in missing details, you'll understand concepts you have trouble with, and you'll be able to pool your resources and divide up the labor.

Starting a study group is easier once you get into your major; you'll see the same people in class after class, but, as a freshman, you may not know a soul in your 8:30 a.m. biology class. If that's the case, wait until the first exam is approaching and ask lab partners, the people you sit next to in class, the guy/girl you recognize from your dorm, or whomever if they want to join a group. You may also use social media or a course web page to find or start a study group.

A good study group is filled with students who are motivated to succeed and take the group seriously. A good study group has at least one organizer to plan meetings and manage a group text/message thread. It's great if you can get weekly meetings going, especially as the term gets closer to finals.

Group size is up to you. I recommend more than two and fewer than eight people. The larger the group, the more likely you are to end up with a lot of sidebar conversations and distractions. Don't be afraid of including a student who is less prepared, so long as that person is serious. You'll learn more by trying to help them. There are always frustrations in working with a group, just remind yourself that their grade is their grade.

Resources

Evernote Notes & Collaboration	Evernote.com Apple & Android App Store
Quizlet Flashcards	Quizlet.com
Study Hacks Cal Newport	calnewport.com/blog/
Anki Multimedia Flashcards	apps.ankiweb.net

23 ACE TESTS & ASSIGNMENTS

You go to class, you study, and somehow your professors have to evaluate how much you learned. Hence assessments: quizzes, tests, papers, presentations, and projects. There's no way around it; however, you can survive and thrive with reasonably little stress if you approach things systematically.

Here are some guidelines that work no matter how you're assessed.

Prioritize – Not all assignments are created equal, and your time is not infinite. You should have enough time to get things done if you manage your time well. There will, however, be times where you'll have to squeak through an assignment in order to focus on an assignment/test that's more important. Criteria for prioritizing assignments include your current grade in the course, the weight of the assignment in your course grade, and the importance of the course.

Give Yourself Time – Estimate how long it will take you to complete the assignment or prepare for the test. Budget a reasonable amount of time each day for as long as you'll need. For example, it's good practice to prepare for a *minimum* of an hour a day for at *least* a week leading up to an exam.

Give Yourself More Time – Double any time estimate you make. It's very likely you've underestimated the work, overestimated your efficiency or both. It's also highly likely you'll run into a snag or two along the way.

Collaborate – Form study groups. Have a classmate look over your paper, presentation, or project. A quality reviewer will—almost always—uncover something that you missed.

Use Your Professor/TA – Professors don't intend assessments to be black boxes. Go to office hours and discuss your ideas, your drafts, or your progress. Ask for advice on any tough spots you hit. You professor will even give you some help in the run-up to a test—they won't give you the test questions, but they'll make it clear what they think is important.

Don't Cheat – It's on every syllabus, they talk about it at orientation, and your professors warn you not to. Don't do it. Buying papers seldom works because of plagiarism detecting software. Presentations and other written output can be checked using that method, and they are also more memorable and easily found on Google. To be very honest, you may get away with cheating on a test. But, if you get caught, you will get an unforgivable F (think a scarlet letter on your transcript), you may get kicked out of your program, or you may be expelled from your college. An expulsion is harder to overcome and lingers longer than many criminal convictions.

<u>Writing Strategies</u>

I see a remarkable amount of bad writing from college students and graduates. Not only does it make me cringe as I have to decipher their meaning, I feel a little bad for the writer because an inability to write will seriously hamper you. Regardless of your career goals, you'll have to write professional emails to colleagues, customers, and bosses.

Pay attention to developing your writing skills, but, to be frank, you'll need to learn how to write somewhat differently in the workplace than in your academic career (in college you're trying to sound smart and probably trying to pad length). Even though I write to earn a significant portion of my living, I consider my writing workmanlike at best. I don't think I'm an expert, but I do have a set of priorities for writing, which I think are broadly applicable to academic and professional settings.

1. **Clarity** – Your writing needs to convey the information you want it to convey. For papers, those are usually facts and your own conjectures, but if you're studying creative writing you'll be trying to evoke emotions in the reader.

2. **Brevity** – Good writing gets in, gets the job done, and gets out. Extra words are the enemy. If you've ever felt like an author was

wasting your time (I promise I didn't do it on purpose) it's likely because they're going long and their sentences need trimmed. They may also be repeating themselves.

3. **Tone** – You need to maintain a professional tone and a third person perspective unless the assignment calls for otherwise. Avoid contractions and slang. Also watch out for making unsubstantiated statements or generalizations. Also, avoid clichés like the plague (see what I did there?).

Writing Strategies & Tips

Outline – I love outlining even very short writing projects. The time you spend outlining will be more than made up for by the time and frustration you save while writing. I also offer my personal guarantee that you'll produce stronger, more coherent writing. Check out the resources section of this chapter for a great article on outlining.

Be Careful with Your Sources – Make sure you follow the guidelines for sources. Wikipedia is almost never acceptable, but it's a great place to get an idea of your topic, and you may find sources in the footnotes.

Do one thing at a time – you can't adequately organize, write, and edit. Just get the first draft down on paper, citing as you go, and then come back and edit your writing. Give yourself permission to be bad on the first draft. As Hemingway said, "The first draft of anything is shit."

Stay on Target – Beware of going on page after page on some relatively minor point. Keeping on the main idea is much easier if you've done a good job with an outline.

Finish with the Beginning – Beginnings are hard to write. To make life easier, write your body first, your conclusion next, and your intro last. You know those meta chapters at the beginning of each section in this book? Guess what I wrote last.

Be Specific – A lot of writing is very general, and that's fine for a conversational tone (like this book), but it doesn't work well with papers. Use quantifiable statements, clear relationships between facts/ideas, and support any assertion you make.

Use Grammarly – I don't like Google Docs, and I dread using it each year when application season comes around. Microsoft Word is better, but it still misses quite a bit. I recommend using Grammarly to check your grammar—the free version is fine.

Read Like You're the Reader – The ability to put yourself in the reader's shoes is what distinguishes great writers from good writers. When you read your work, try to imagine that you have no idea what argument you're making or what your perspective is. If you're writing for an audience that has little or no knowledge of your subject, then make sure you account for that as well. That generally won't be a problem as you'll be writing for professors who are experts in their field.

Test Prep Strategies

If you paid attention to the last chapter, test preparation will be much easier. That said, you're not perfect, and studying won't always go smoothly. Here are some recommendations that work for all courses.

Have a Plan – It's inefficient to study all material equally. Put yourself in the shoes of your professor; think about what they consider important. What did they emphasize in class? What did they put on the board? What got theme excited? Use your knowledge of the professor to help prioritize your topics. Use the end of chapter objectives and questions from your text to do the same.

Use Practice Tests – If you're given practice tests, great. If you aren't, make them yourself (see the previous chapter).

Break it Up – Ideally, you'll start a week (or more) before each exam. It's more effective, less stressful, and makes your life—and grades—much better. Studying an hour a day for a week is better than twelve or fourteen hours at once.

Cramming – Ok, so you didn't listen to all that great advice from the previous chapters, and now you're behind the academic 8-ball. It's almost inevitable that you'll have to cram at some point. Here are some suggestions for making life better. For tips on how to physically endure an all-nighter check out the chapter on *Eating, Sleeping, & Taking Care of Yourself*. Seriously, check it out.

✓ Take Breaks, either use a Pomodoro Timer and take a five-minute break after 25-minutes and a 15-minute break every two hours. Get up and walk around, definitely take a break from screen time.

✓ Use active learning strategies. The more active you are, the better your results will be (see previous chapter).

✓ Focus on the big picture. If you're cramming, it's likely because you're behind. Focus on getting the most important topics right, because that's where the most points will be.

✓ Use practice tests. Notice how much I mention practice tests? It's because they are that important.

✓ Try chunking the material onto notecards or in paragraphs. You're much more likely to remember the concepts that way. Quizlet works for this as well.

✓ Change things up. If you're studying anatomy, don't always start at the front of the skull, start at the back, or the side. You can even change up things that have chronology (just be mindful not to mix up your dates).

Presentation Strategies

From time to time, you'll have to get up in front of your peers and professor and give a short talk, usually accompanied by a slideshow. If you're terrified of public speaking, don't be. **I'll tell you a secret, no one is paying very close attention nor are they judging you**. They're busy thinking about their own presentation, what they're going to have for lunch, or who they want to hook up with. Here's how to succeed in a presentation.

Keep it (relatively) simple – It's easy to get lost in the details. You want to give a presentation that shows you have command of the material. To do so, focus on the most powerful points and adequately support them. You want to make a coherent argument or tell a coherent story, without a lot of junk.

Practice & Prepare – This is even more important if you're nervous. Practice the presentation in the shower, in front of a mirror, etc. If you've got a case of stage fright, practice it until it bores you to tears. It'll keep the nerves at bay when it comes time to deliver the real thing.

Find Test Listeners – The best test listeners are people in your class, but you can substitute people who have taken the course, people in your major, or even people who have no idea what you're doing.

Do it in Office Hours – Hey, here's a great idea, what if you could give your presentation to the person who will grade you before they grade you? You can, in most cases, and I encourage you to.

Look Good/Feel Good – Make sure you get some rest, have something to eat, don't party the night before, and wear something halfway decent to a presentation. The better you look, the more confident you'll feel.

Talk & Don't Read –If you've practiced, you should be able to do it without cue cards or an outline, but you can bring either. If you freeze up, pause and compose yourself. When you stop talking it may seem like forever, but it really will only be a few seconds.

Eye Contact – Make eye contact with your audience. If you have trouble with that, look at the top of their heads (they won't know the difference).

Group Project Strategies

Choose Wisely – If you have a choice of who is in your group, try to find people who match, or exceed, your level of motivation.

Be Positive – Don't talk about group members to other group members and make any criticism constructive. It can be hard to be positive at times, but being negative will yield you nothing.

Agree on How to Communicate – Form a group text, whatsapp thingamajig, or however it is your group want to stay in contact. Make sure everyone is on it, and put all official business through it for everyone to see.

Use Calendar Invites – Using calendar invites will help prevent people from being late or no-showing your meetings. Even if people don't keep a calendar, receiving a calendar invite lets them know it, and you, are serious.

Take the Lead – But don't dominate the meetings or try and coerce others to your point of view. It will create hostility, and even if you get your way, everyone else will put less effort into the project. Your role is more like the head of a committee than captain of a ship.

Or, Don't Take the Lead – If you don't want to be a leader/organizer, then don't be one. Contribute to the conversation, work hard, and stand up for your viewpoint on how the project should proceed. You don't always have to be a leader, and you don't always have to be a follower.

Accept Consensus – If a decision is made, go with it. You'll waste time and deteriorate the group dynamic by relentlessly holding on to your point.

Resources

Grammarly Grammar & Style Check	Grammarly.com
Purdue OWL Style & Citation Help	owl.english.purdue.edu/owl
Slack Group Projects	Slack.com
Asana Group Projects	Asana.com

24 DEAL WITH PROFESSORS

<u>Six Rules of Etiquette</u>

Regardless of what you're trying to get out of your professor, you should follow some basic, mannerly rules. (If you're looking for advice on dealing with the professor who is your advisor, check out the chapter on *Dealing with Advisers*).

Talking to students is part of a professor's job. That said, *they do not work for you*. You need to treat them respectfully, particularly if you're asking for a favor.

1. **Be Respectful.** To start with, use the right title. If it's a PhD, PsyD, EdD, or MD, use "doctor" or "professor." If the instructor does not hold a doctoral degree, "mister," "miss," or "professor" all work fine. In general, never call a woman "missus" unless you know she is married. Typically, professors list their educational credentials on the syllabus. Err on the side of caution if you are unsure, you're unlikely to offend someone by calling them a doctor, and professor is always safe.

   If you're sending an email, it needs to be businesslike (check out the resource section for examples). If you go to office hours be polite, respectful, and get to the point. This goes double if you're upset about a grade or you want some special accommodation. Frankly, I could have lumped all six tips in this list under the heading of "be respectful."

2. **Go to Class**. Try not to miss class. Your life has entered a whole new dimension. For the first time, you won't be directly and immediately punished for some misdeed, but you'll build up a tab which costs

performance, opportunities, and makes you anxious. So, go to class unless it's unavoidable. One more thing, *put your phone away.*

Your behavior in class is important. I teach online, and I can tell when someone is looking at his or her phone, even if I can't see the phone. Your professors can too. Don't fall asleep and don't talk to your neighbor throughout class.

3. **Participate.** You don't have to sit in the front row, but sit somewhere where you can see, be seen, and it's easy for you to pay attention. Answer questions, ask questions (if you have the question, at least one other person does), and contribute. Don't take it too far: don't continuously interrupt to ask questions, it throws off the professor and his/her goal of getting through X amount of material that day. Before you ask about a due date or something, make sure it hasn't been made clear in the syllabus or other instructions.

4. **Keep Appointments.** If you make an appointment to see your professor, you need to keep it. That appointment should take priority over any competing obligation, barring emergency.

5. **Have a Purpose.** If you go see your professor, have a real reason for doing so. Otherwise you risk looking like you're trying to curry favor. That said, if you're in the area, there's nothing wrong with popping in and saying a quick hello.

6. **Be Honest.** Professors get lied to **all the time**, and you won't fool them. Just be honest, they'll understand that people make mistakes. They're probably more likely to help you if you come clean than otherwise.

From Your Professor's Point of View

Professors are People Too – Professors don't always get treated great by students. They are, at times, threatened with legal action or even physically threatened by upset students. Treat your professor with the respect due to their position and the respect due to them as a human being.

Their Course is Important – There's nothing that will sink your hopes of a grade appeal faster than, "But this isn't my major." You took the class, and it's your responsibility to take it seriously. Aside from being ineffective, it's also insulting.

Your GPA is <u>Your</u> Responsibility – Your grades are your own business, but professors want to help you. They do not, however, want to bail you out or be your saving grace.

Deadlines are <u>Not</u> Suggestions – Deadlines are deadlines. If you need an extension, you should have a good reason. You should also ask for extensions as far as possible before the due date.

Communication Methods

Many professors list their communication preferences on the syllabus. Try and communicate with them according to their wishes. If they don't get back to you, don't take it personally just try a different method.

Before/After Class – If you have a quick question that may be off-topic for the lecture, ask it before or after class.

Email – When emailing your professor, use their title and compose the email in a business-like manner. Avoid slang, abbreviations, contractions, and the like. Also use a closing. Be careful not to phrase your questions as demands.

Office Hours – Go to office hours for help or more involved questions. If you're asking for a favor, it's best to do that in person.

Communication Purpose

Questions – If you have a quick material or logistical question, ask it before, during, or after class. Make sure you've taken a look at the course materials if your question is about an assignment or assessment. Otherwise you may look unprepared. If you have a question that will require a lengthy answer, ask after class or during office hours. Try to understand the material before you go to your professor, you'll get more out of the interaction, and your professor will have a favorable opinion of you.

Grades – Didn't do as well as you thought you would on an assignment or assessment? Speak to the professor about your grade, but act like an adult. These conversations are best held in office hours. Ask your professor how you can perform better on assignments or if they have any study suggestions for you. For example, if you were disappointed in your grade on a paper, you could say something like, "I thought I did a pretty good job following the instructions and grading rubric, can you give me some pointers on how to approach papers like this in the future?" Before you go to your professor, make sure you've read and attempted to understand their notes/annotations. It's better to have a conversation clearing up what they meant by their notes than a broad conversation about the grade.

If you think your professor made a mistake, remember it's a mistake. It is exceedingly unlikely that a professor is trying to be unfair. It's also somewhat unlikely they made a grading error. Phrase your question like, "I don't understand how I missed this question, can you explain it please?" or, "I thought I cited my sources correctly and chose appropriate sources, can you explain where I made mistakes?"

Advice – It's great to ask your professor about how to do well in their course. Professors teach the same course over and over, and they'll have noticed patterns in their successful students. Aside from the obvious (organization, showing up to class, participating, etc.), they may have a couple of tidbits that you wouldn't think of otherwise.

You may have questions for your professor that are outside the realm of his/her course. Feel free to ask professors about their research (if you're genuinely interested), opportunities for the summer, or what classes to take outside of your major that may relate to their course(s) or would be generally beneficial. I would skip asking your political science professor, "who is the best professor to take international studies from?" Professors are unlikely to pick among their close colleagues within the department.

Advising – If you want your professor to be your advisor, *ask during office hours.* At many institutions, professors take fewer undergraduate advisees than lecturers, so if your professor says that he/she can't take you on, don't take it personally. For advice more advice on selecting and working with an advisor, check out the next chapter on *Advisors.*

Social Calls – If you happen to be in the department, it doesn't hurt to say hi to your professor. If you're in a large class, or it's near the beginning of the semester, introduce yourself first. "Hi Dr. Jones, I'm Sally from your 9 a.m. Intro to Archeology course." If something has piqued your interest, bring it up. Most professors want to talk to students, and, in general, people like it if/when you share an interest. That said, if you need to talk business, particularly if you're asking for a favor, keep it on point.

Extension/Missed Assignments/Tests – Ask during office hours, unless it's an emergency, then do so by email. If you're missing a test, you need to contact them before the test starts. Do your best to contact them as soon as possible. Be prepared to provide documentation as to why you're missing.

Picking Professors

Online Reviews – You're probably keenly aware of the problems with online reviews. Unlike departmental reviews (the bubble sheets that you fill in at the end of the semester), online reviews you find on sites like ratemyprofessor.com are from a self-selecting sample. It's not going to be a cross-section of all students who take the class. As such, online reviews tend to be extreme, written by reviewers who are overly positive or (more likely) overly negative. I don't think there's anything wrong with looking at the reviews but don't believe everything you read.

Peers – Are, generally, a much more reliable source of information. Typically, you know something about the student you're asking: how hard they study, how good they are at the subject, their goals, and so on. You can use your knowledge of your peer(s) to filter the review that they give you. If you don't know anyone who is ahead of you in school, check out some of the student organizations relating to major, like the American Chemical Society or the Society or Women Engineers. Alternatively, you can ask RA's in your dorm who you know have the same major.

YouTube/Posted Resources – Professors often have lectures available on YouTube or other resources on the web. Recorded lectures give you a good idea of the professor's teaching style as do the tone and nature of any free resources they provide. If the professor took the initiative (versus the department) to post materials or lectures, it's a strong indication that this is a professor who really cares about teaching undergraduates.

Sit in on Classes – If you plan on taking Organic Chemistry in the fall, sit in on a few classes with different professors (assuming your college has more than one professor teaching organic chemistry). Don't worry about understanding the material, pay attention to the attitude of the students in the class, the pacing of the professor, and how he/she interacts with students. If everyone seems miserable or detached, it's a bad sign.

Bad Professors

You'll have at least one bad professor in college. But remember, bad and tough are two different things. Bad professors are uninterested, unclear, unfair, and/or unorganized. The best way to deal with a bad professor is don't. Do your best to avoid them by doing your homework, or get out quickly if you can.

Unfortuantely, you can't always avoid a bad professor, particularly at smaller schools. If you're stuck with the professor, you'll have to do your best. With a bad professor, communication with your professor is even more important. Remember, you're going to have to be the one that changes—they are unlikely to.

Give it some time, and make sure you go to office hours at least once before you quit. For more advice on when to drop a course check out the chapter on *Bad Test, Bad Class, Bad Semester.*

Resources

Grammarly	Grammarly.com
Grammar & Style Check	
Purdue OWL	owl.english.purdue.edu/owl
Style & Citation Help	
Slack	Slack.com
Group Projects	
Asana	Asana.com
Group Projects	

25 TAKE CARE OF YOURSELF
Self-Care, Stress, & Success

I think of the work version of me as a tool, like a knife. I like to cook, and I have one of those serious chef knives. It's made of carbon steel, so I have to be careful to dry it when I wash it (unlike stainless, it'll discolor or rust). I also use a steel on it and sharpen it regularly. Once a year, or so, I take it to a professional to put an edge on it.

At least that's how it worked before I had my daughter. I'm super busy now with work and being a single parent, so my poor knife languishes. It's dull which makes it hard to use, and I've even cut myself a couple of times (dull knives are dangerous knives).

Life is full of competing interests, and I'm guilty of letting my responsibilities pull me into too many pieces to where nothing is left over. When that happens I get dull like my knife. My teaching is off, my writing is off, I lose things, I forget appointments, everything feels harder. In short, I get less done and what I get done is of poorer quality.

But it's easy to fix. All I need to do is engage in self-care. I need to go to the gym, make an elaborate meal, go to Costco (we all have our own definitions of self-care), or spend some time with my friends or my daughter without being preoccupied with "what needs done."

I think most people are like me, to a greater or lesser degree. One part of adulthood that I think you should figure out in college is how you can protect yourself from your various identities and responsibilities.

In the *Mental Health* chapter I talk briefly about my own issues with Bipolar II disorder. It's an important part of my life, and one I wish I had handled differently, so I talk about it in order to help people who may be reticent to seek help. I strongly encourage you to remember that how you feel determines how you see the world and yourself. Be kind to yourself.

128

For me, self-care involves the gym, a hobby I like, a change of scenery, taking care of my mental health, and being with people I care about. The specifics of what self-care looks like for you will be different, but I think it should include several domains: your physical health, your mental health, a passion for something that's completely unrelated to your career goals, and people you love.

That's what self-care is to me, and I can tell you that if I don't engage in self-care, I'm much more stressed and I'm less successful at whatever I'm trying to do, including being a Dad.

In This Section

Exercise, Sleeping, & Eating – You don't have to pump iron, or become a yoga teacher to benefit from exercise. You don't have to go vegan to eat reasonably. And 5 hours of sleep a night is good for no one.

Student Health Services – I talk about what your college may offer as well as health insurance. More importantly, I discuss some of the preventative services that colleges offer. It's my sincere hope that you develop an attitude to cultivating your health, versus treating sickness.

Mental Health Services – I discuss how counselors can help you, even if you're just stressed as well as symptoms of mental health conditions.

Accommodations for Disability – If you have a physical, emotional, or learning disability, accommodations are vital for your success. It's not about how well you do; it's about how well you could do.

26 EAT, SLEEP, EXERCISE

It's easy to put-off living a healthy lifestyle in college. Instead of thinking about the superficial aspects of health and wellness, **think about a healthy lifestyle as a crucial component of human performance and mental wellbeing.** Only 50% of college students eat a diet that's nutritionally balanced, 48.7% of students have iron deficient anemia, 46.3% get enough sleep, 38% are obese, and only 34% exercise frequently.

Eating Well Improves Performance & Wellbeing

It's tough to eat healthy in college. While dining halls have made strides to be healthier, they still have plenty of unhealthy options available. Guess what? The unhealthy options are more tempting.

But students who live off-campus are no better off. Students living off-campus shop for their groceries, but their priorities are usually cheap and easy. Unfortunately, cheap and easy food tends to be unhealthy. Check out the Resources section of this chapter for a guide to eating healthy in college. Here are some guidelines for making healthier choices:

Eat Breakfast – It's common for college students to skip breakfast. It's really easy and awfully tempting to wake up 15 minutes before class, throw on your hoodie and walk to campus. As someone who has always had a tough time getting up in the morning, I empathize. There are workarounds, however. Keep some fruit or bars in your room and take them with you as you walk. **If you have an exam that day, make sure you eat breakfast.**

Students who eat breakfast have an easier time regulating their weight and have better micronutrient and vitamin levels. Furthermore, students who eat breakfast are more likely to be physically active, have a higher fitness level, and reduced illness frequency.

Eating to be Productive – Whenever I eat too much, I'm sluggish and have a hard time focusing. Honestly, I do best when I'm a little bit hungry. While your experience may vary, eating a huge lunch that's heavy in carbohydrates and fat will signal your body to focus on digestion and not on getting more food. You'll be less alert and have a harder time thinking. You aren't out hunting and gathering, but the "get more food" drive is a big part of what gets us to be productive.

Eating to Feel Better – Sometimes a pint of ice cream is just what you need, but it's a short-term bump. Diets that are lower in refined sugars and saturated fats reduce the risk of depression between 25 and 35%. People who eat healthier tend to have lower stress and anxiety levels and more positive mental outlooks. You may also want to consider a probiotic supplement; research has shown probiotics can improve your mental wellbeing.

Strategies for Eating Better

Don't Grocery Shop Hungry – I always make bad decisions when I grocery shop hungry, not only for my diet but my wallet as well. Most people do, a hungry brain is too focused on immediate gratification to make good decisions.

Don't Pick Your Meal Hungry – This sounds a little silly, but don't walk into the dining hall until you know what you're going to eat (menus are available online). When you're hungry your self-control is at a low point, and you're more likely to choose an unhealthy food.

Pack Snacks – Pack some healthy snacks wherever you go. Nuts, dried fruit, bars (check the sugar content), are all good options. It's a bit of a paradox, but eating more often tends to make people eat less, because the blood glucose level doesn't tank. Going hungry isn't going to keep off weight, but eating smaller portions throughout the day will. Do yourself a favor though, and keep an eye on your portion size.

Track What You Eat – Most people have no idea what or how much they consume on a day-to-day basis. Even if you're not trying to lose weight, you can use a calorie/nutrient counting app to keep track of what you're taking in. I use the LoseIt app every day, and I'm not trying to lose weight.

Treat Yourself – I'm a big believer in moderation. Give yourself permission to eat terribly from time-to-time. You can set a quota for this, as fitness buffs do, or just be prudent (tracking can really come in handy here).

Disordered Eating & Eating Disorders

In the chapter on *Mental Health* I go into detail about eating disorders and disordered eating. If you feel you may have a problematic relationship with food and body image, please check it out. Please seek help if you need it.

Getting the Right Amount of Sleep Improves Everything

People love to brag about how little sleep they're getting. It's the kind of boast that shows how tough and how dedicated they are. It's also foolish. **Sleep is not time wasted; sleep is not a luxury; sleep makes us happier, healthier, and more productive.**

Seventy percent of college students aren't sleeping enough, and half of students report daytime sleepiness. College students suffer from lack of sleep for the same reasons other adults do: they go to bed too late and wake up too early. Your sleep-wake cycle isn't entirely your fault. Your circadian rhythms change after puberty and, as a result, teenagers and young adults feel more awake in the evening, thus making it harder to fall asleep.

There is ample evidence that getting enough sleep is crucial for your academic performance. One study found that students who got six or fewer hours of sleep had an average GPA of 2.74, while students who had an adequate amount of sleep had an average GPA of 3.24.

Unfortunately, students get busier later in the semester and, consequently, sleep less. While you'll always be busier later in the term, good time management and good sleep practices will make your life so much easier and your grades so much better.

Different people require different amounts of sleep. For some, six hours is sufficient while others may require nine hours. Tracking your sleep can let you know how much sleep you're actually getting. Signs of sleep deprivation include sleeping for more than two extra hours during the weekend and feeling tired and irritable throughout the day. Try 7 -8 hours for a few weeks and see what happens.

Quality of Sleep Matters

Depending on who you ask, the quality of your sleep may be even more important than how long you sleep. Sleep quality is very subjective, but there are some criteria: being asleep 85%+ of the time in bed, falling asleep in 30 minutes or less, and waking up no more than once a night. If you're using a wearable device, like a Fitbit, it will track your sleep-wake cycles. I'm not always sold on the reliability of my Fitbit for things like heart rate and sleep, but I think it's a helpful guidepost.

Judging the Length & Quality of Your Sleep

Pittsburgh Sleep Index – The Pittsburgh Sleep Index is a self-administered survey that can give you some insight into how you're sleeping and what helps or hinders your rest. I've provided a link in the Resources section.

Trackers – If you have a Fitbit, Apple watch, or other wearable, pay attention to what it tells you about your sleep. Remember, you want to have 7+ hours of total sleep and few interruptions.

How To Fix Your Lack of Sleep or Your Lacking Sleep

Track – Use a tracker, paper log, spreadsheet, or a regular evaluation with the Pittsburgh Sleep Index to track how you're sleeping. The more data you collect, the better idea you'll get about what works and does not work for you.

Call it Quits – You have to be able to say, "enough is enough" and cut off your work for the evening (provided something isn't due at 8 a.m. the next morning). There is almost always more work can do, and so waiting until you're "finished with everything" is illogical. It's a tradeoff, and sacrificing sleep for extra productivity is a poor trade. It's like borrowing money from a loan shark; in the short-run you get the cash you need, in the long-run you lose a finger.

Caffeine – Caffeine is tricky; it has a half life of about five or six hours. Meaning half of the caffeine in the cup of coffee, tea, or Red Bull you drank at 6 p.m. will still be in your system at midnight. Most of the effects of caffeine are felt in the first five or six hours, but caffeine can interrupt your sleep after that time.

Do your best to stop your caffeine consumption in the mid-afternoon. If you have trouble cutting back your evening caffeine consumption (hey, caffeine is a drug) then start by substituting less caffeinated drinks to step down.

Stimulants – Adderall, Dexedrine, and Ritalin are increasingly popular with students who believe they are performance enhancing drugs. Please remember that these are amphetamines and you shouldn't take them unless they are prescribed to you. They can severely disrupt your sleep schedule, appetite, and may have other unpleasant and dangerous side effects.

That said, they produce wonderful results for those who are prescribed them. If you take a stimulant ADHD medication and have trouble sleeping, consult a doctor.

Alcohol – Alcohol is a depressant and will help you fall asleep, **but at a cost that's not worth paying**. Alcohol disrupts the latter half of the sleep cycle, preventing you from falling into deep sleep and keeping you in a REM state. As such, you're likely to wake up tired, somewhat dehydrated, and with a bit of a headache.

Approximately 11% of college students report using alcohol as a sleep aid. If you do this regularly, talk to a doctor. You could be developing a serious substance abuse problem, alcoholism. A medical professional can help you find healthier ways to fall and stay asleep.

Sleep Hygiene
I find the term sleep hygiene awkward, but I can't deny that it is descriptive. **Sleep hygiene is putting as much thought into ending your day as you put into beginning it**. Here's the trick, sleep hygiene does not work unless you **practice it consistently**, and it may not be effective for you for the first few weeks you try.

Technology – That nice blue-white iPhone screen is keeping you awake. Screens produce wavelengths of light that are pretty close to daylight, which suppresses melatonin, a hormone that helps regulate your sleep. Make sure your phone is on night mode and try to avoid excessive screen time for a few hours before bed. Don't leave Netflix on while you go to sleep. It'll take you longer to fall asleep, and once you do, you'll have poorer quality sleep.

Natural Light – Exposure to natural light is incredibly important in regulating your sleep/wake cycle. If you live in a more northern environment and find yourself particularly affected by the dark winter days, try using a full spectrum light during the day. The full spectrum light emulates natural light well enough to help your natural rhythms. That said, don't use one at night; they can seriously interfere with your sleep.

Schedule – Try to go to bed at the same time every night—at *least* during the week. On the other end, try to get up at the same time every morning. Your bedtime/wake time will fluctuate some, but try to keep it within half an hour or so.

Bedtime Alarm – I use bedtime alarms from time-to-time, and I probably should do so more often. I use them when I know I'll have to wake up earlier than usual, when I'm likely to be engrossed in a task that will be hard to break away from, or when I'm reading a particularly good novel. That said, I'm somewhat older than most of you, so I have more of a routine built up. So you may want to try this on a daily basis to establish a good habit.

Naps – There's nothing wrong with taking naps regularly. In fact, over half of high academic achievers nap often while only 29% of low academic achievers do so. That said, keep your naps limited to half an hour. Otherwise, you'll disrupt your sleep in the evening.

Class Scheduling – One study found that boarding school students benefited from a later start time, gaining 45 minutes of sleep by starting half an hour later. Almost ironically, the later start time resulted in students going to bed earlier. Some people are morning people, and some are night owls (I'm the latter). It turns out that it's very difficult or impossible to change from a night owl to a morning person or vice versa, so set up your life accordingly.

Therapy – Many colleges offer email based therapy for insomnia or poor sleep. If you're having trouble, please investigate what resources are available to you. Sleep therapy is typically Cognitive Behavior Therapy based, meaning that they're interested in helping you create rational thinking patterns and healthy habits.

Exercise – Students who exercise sleep better. You don't have to work out to the point of exhaustion; any routine will work. Exercise is particularly effective for people who have chronic insomnia.

All Nighters

Staying awake all night impairs your memory and judgment equivalent to a blood-alcohol level of .10%, above the threshold for legal intoxication. No matter what I say here, you all will pull at least one all-nighter in college. Here's how to do it in the most productive way.

- ✓ **Nap Before** – Naps before all-nighters are incredibly helpful in giving you some energy while also increasing your memory, retention, and ability to focus. Experts say that the best length for the pre-all-nighter nap is 90 minutes.

- ✓ **Light** – You'll want to be in a well-lit place, and, if possible, use a full-spectrum light. Light will keep the melatonin at bay and trick your body into thinking it is still daytime.

- ✓ **Keep it Cool** – You'll be more alert if your surroundings are a little less than 70 degrees. You probably don't have control over the library's thermostat or maybe even your room's, so focus on avoiding a super cozy feeling. Cozy makes for drowsy.

- ✓ **Snack Healthy** – Opt out of candy and sugary snacks. While you may get a short burst of energy from sweets, it doesn't last, and you don't want your blood glucose level to yo-yo. When it comes to all-nighters, eat snacks that have staying power. Nuts, fruit, and lean protein are ideal.

- ✓ **Stay Hydrated** – Caffeine is dehydrating. Drink plenty of water or sports drinks to counterbalance the effect.

- ✓ **Watch the Caffeine** – Go easy on the caffeine or you'll find yourself anxious and unable to concentrate. More caffeine isn't always the answer. Remember, the effects of caffeine last 5+ hours, and once you consume caffeine, it takes around half an hour to start to take effect and the effect peaks between 2 – 4 hours. Be careful, caffeine is dangerous at high levels.

- ✓ **Take Breaks** – You can use Pomodoros during all-nighters (See: *Time Management*). If you don't use Pomodoros, set a timer to ding every 45 minutes. When the timer goes off, get up from your seat and take a walk for five minutes. Taking a screen break reduces eyestrain, refreshes you, and improves your alertness and ability to focus.

Getting Out of Bed

If you're having trouble waking up, look at how and when you're going to bed. It's very likely that you're not getting enough sleep, you're drinking alcohol too often, or you're impairing the quality of your sleep with having the TV on. Start by working on sleep hygiene.

If improving your sleep routine doesn't work, think about how you plan to start the morning. It's always easy to tell yourself the night before that you'll hop out of bed, do 50 pushups and dive right into that chemistry you hate. For some people, that works. For others, myself included, you won't get out of bed to make yourself uncomfortable. As trite as it sounds, you need a reason to get out of bed, so think about what will <u>incentivize</u> you to get up when the alarm goes off. Here are some things to try:

- ✓ **Reward Yourself** – Have something to look forward to when you get out of bed. Whether it's a couple of slices of bacon from the cafeteria, coffee, or doing something you fun first thing. I often start the day with some easy mundane task or something I want to do.

- ✓ **Increase Natural Light** – Open your blinds and curtains before you go to bed, particularly on any window facing you while you sleep.

- ✓ **Eat a Nightly Snack** – Sometimes people feel groggy in the morning because they are super hungry after night asleep. A healthy, low-carb snack, works great for many people.

- ✓ **Eat First Thing** – Eating can motivate you to get out of bed, and it's the best way to get your body ready for the day.

✓ **Prep Before Bed** – If you feel like the day is waiting for you, it'll be easier for you to get up and get going. Pack your backpack or bag the night before and put it where it's visible from the bed. Not only will this make getting up easier (hey, one thing is already done), but it will also be a lifesaver in case something you need isn't where you thought it was.

✓ **The Inverted Snooze** – Whenever you hit the snooze button, get out of bed and stand for the next nine minutes. After nine minutes you can get back into bed. Try it out; you'll get the idea.

✓ **Put Some Water by Your Bed** – Some people swear by this. Put a cup or bottle of water next to your bed, so you can have a couple of drinks first thing can be invigorating.

✓ **Experiment with Alarms** – Put your alarm in different locations (always keep it out of arm's reach), try different tones or music, and adjust loudness, etc. Try an alarm that wakes you gradually. You can also check out some of the alarms that require an extra step: one has a flying helicopter that you have to return to its pad before it shuts off, another requires you to put your feet on a mat. These are gimmicky, but it may work for you.

Regardless of what your "out of bed recipe" looks like, it is important that you don't become a chronic snoozer. Repeated snoozing can cause you to fall into deeper sleep and have an even harder time waking. If none of this works well for you, consult a doctor, there may be medical reasons for your difficulty.

Sleep Disorders

Over 25% of college students either have or are at risk for a sleep disorder. Sleep disorders include sleep apnea, insomnia, restless leg symptom, circadian rhythm disorders, and hypersomnia (sleeping too much). If you feel like you may have a sleep disorder, see a doctor.

The Benefits of Exercise

It's easy to take an all-or-nothing approach to exercise: either you look like a personal trainer, or you're a slob. Movies, television, magazines, and ads are filled with incredibly fit and good looking individuals. And in your life— particularly on social media—90% of what you hear about fitness comes from the 10% of people who are, perhaps, too into fitness.

It doesn't have to be this way, and, in fact, it shouldn't. You can find exercise that works for who you are and fits your life, you can get all the benefits of a healthier body, better mind, and more balanced life without going to the extremes of aspiring underwear models.

Academically – GPA rises (it's debated by how much) with the amount of exercise you get. The effect is cumulative up to a point, meaning more exercise is better. Exercise also helps graduation rates; one study showed that regular exercisers are 47% more likely to graduate than their peers. Of course, you can overdo it and actually hurt your GPA (exercise addiction is a real thing, check the Resources section of this chapter).

Mentally – Students who exercise regularly have improved concentration and information retention. In secondary school students, it has been reported that regular exercise makes students more likely to participate.

Emotionally – For some, exercise is as effective as medication for alleviating depression. Regardless of your emotional state, you'll benefit from the mood boost, confidence, and stress relief that exercise gives you. Exercise also gives you a sense of accomplishment and enhanced self-esteem. You may also make a few friends along the way.

Physically – If you exercise, you'll be in better physical shape (obviously). You'll also sleep better, have more energy, and have a much easier time regulating your weight (or losing weight). You'll also get sick less often, and you'll recover from illness more quickly.

Your Student Recreation Center(s)

Colleges have gone to considerable trouble and expense to create state of the art recreation centers for students and staff. It's been a bit of an arms race between schools, as the fitness center can be a shiny selling point to potential students (remember, colleges operate like businesses even though they don't think they do).

You're the beneficiary of all this, as student recreation offerings are more sophisticated and varied than ever before. It's not just treadmills and weights; it's classes, outdoor programs, pools, climbing walls, and more.

Even if you aren't a gym person, check out the recreation center's offerings. I guarantee that you'll find something worth trying.

What Kind of Exercise?

Here are some criteria to help you formulate a plan, but it's all based on one principle: **the best exercise is the one you will do.**

Accessible – Your exercise plan has to fit in your life. You have to be able to access the gym, class, trail, wall, etc. relatively easily, without adding a ton of time or effort to your day. It's best to be independent. If you need someone else for transportation, you'll end up missing twice as many days (the days you would miss plus the days he/she will miss). That said, I like exercising with a partner, it increases accountability and makes things more fun. If you want to exercise with a partner or take a class, your timing may be restricted, so try and build some other aspects of your life around your activity.

Take a good look at how you live your life. If you're not a morning person, waking up extra early to go to the gym is not going to work. You may want to try exercising after your classes and before you study or in a long break between classes.

Comfortable – If you hate a type of exercise or feel like you can't keep up, you're unlikely to persist. Exercise can make you uncomfortable (although it doesn't have to), but you shouldn't dread it. It's far better to exercise at a level you feel comfortable with because you're far more likely to exercise.

Happy & Healthy – Your exercise should fit your personality. I like to go to a gym and do more "workouty" stuff, but my brother rock climbs, kayaks, and mountain bikes. I'm not particularly interested in those activities, so they wouldn't be great choices for me. You can use exercise to teach yourself a new skill, like self-defense or yoga. Exercise can have an artistic or spiritual expression (dance, yoga, etc.). If you're competitive, train for races, join intramurals, or try cross-fit.

You'll need to change things up to keep exercise interesting. Alter your routine, or, even better, try something radically different. There's no harm in taking a yoga class if you're a former offensive lineman. You may not like a lot of things that you try but that's OK. (I do think you should try things more than once, most things are awkward the first time). By trying something new you'll get a better idea of what fitness looks like to you and it fits in your life.

Fits Your Personality – Are you looking for competition, time alone, or a group dynamic? Everyone has different preferences. While I've taken jiu-jitsu and participated in team sports in the past, I generally prefer to exercise alone. You can find quizzes online to tell you your "exercise personality", but I think them a poor substitute for trying things out.

Fits Your Goals – If you have a specific fitness goal in mind, that's wonderful! Use your goal setting tools (see the chapter on *Goal Setting*) to help you achieve it. If you don't have any particular end-goal in mind, set a goal of being physically active (more on this in the following section).

How to Get Started

Set Goals – What are your objectives? Do you want to maintain weight, get in better shape, or feel better? Set a goal or goals based on your objectives. Remember, quantitative goals are better than qualitative goals, but qualitative goals can be part of the equation.

Make a Plan – Keep it simple and realistic. Figure out when exercise will fit best into your life and put it on your calendar. If you have trouble getting out the door, try creating a new habit (see the chapter on *Habit Formation* for more).

Start Slow – I often see new faces at the gym who are exercising to the point of misery. I don't see those people back at the gym for a long time, if ever. If you're miserable while you're exercising and you're terrifically sore for days after, you're unlikely to keep it up. Cut yourself some slack.

Take a Class – Classes are great for trying new types of exercise, and they also make it easier to get a thorough workout (you don't have to plan it out yourself). You won't like all of them, but you have a good chance of finding something that fits you.

Take a Course – Most colleges offer for credit courses (usually one hour) on swimming, weightlifting, yoga, and so on. Some colleges require some a PE credit as part of their general education requirements. Regardless, these courses are a good way to pick up some fitness skills and diversify your course load.

Join a Club – If you're an outdoor sports enthusiast or you enjoy specialized sports—fencing for example—there's probably a club for that. Go to a meeting and check it out. It doesn't matter if you're a complete novice. Check out the chapter on *Getting Involved* for more.

Find a Friend – A workout partner is great for accountability and motivation. It makes exercise more fun because of the camaraderie and the shared experience. A few colleges pair up students with peers who have similar fitness goals or sports interests. The idea is to match you with someone who can help you attain your fitness goals, and, hopefully, you can build a friendship.

Exercise Dependence & Addiction

Exercise dependence and addiction is a very real and very dangerous thing. Exercise dependence and addiction often occur with an eating disorder or disordered eating. Indicators of exercise addiction include

- An increase in the volume, frequency, duration, or intensity of exercise that is harmful.
- Not exercising creates difficulties in living daily life.
- Withdrawal symptoms including anxiety, restlessness, depression, and guilt.
- Exercising against medical advice or without regard to injury.

In the resources section of this chapter, I've included a questionnaire to help you determine whether your relationship with exercise is healthy or harmful. As always, I believe that if you think you need help, you need help.

Resources

Eating Healthy Taylor Share	nerdfitness.com/blog/a-college-guide-to-eating-healthy/
LoseIt Weight Management	Apple & Android App Store
Pittsburgh Sleep Index Questionnaire	opapc.com/uploads/documents/PSQI.pdf
Exercise Addiction Elizabeth Licorish	phillyvoice.com/what-its-survive-exercise-addiction/
Exercise Dependence Questionnaire	sciencenordic.com/test-yourself-are-you-addicted-exercise

27 KNOW YOUR STUDENT HEALTH SERVICES

Student health services provide free or low-cost medical care. They may or may not require private insurance, Medicaid, or enrollment in a student health plan (more on that later this chapter). A 2010 survey of colleges reported that 91% of colleges provided some form of medical services to students. Interestingly, there was no correlation between the size of the college/university and the amount and variety of services offered.

A quick Google search will tell you what services your institution offers. **Mental health and preventative services may be part of a separate department, and they may not be listed on the medical site.** Some schools have counseling *within* the student health services department as well as *independent* of the student health services department.

Insurance

I cannot overemphasize the importance of health insurance. If you break a leg, are hospitalized, or go to the ER, you will find yourself with a crippling bill unless you are insured. If you are uninsured and have a chronic condition, your medication be more expensive, and your condition will not be managed as well because you'll lack adequate care. Additionally, many colleges require that you have health insurance.

If you're relatively young, you can stay on your parents plan until the age of 26. If you plan to stay on your parent's plan, make sure that the coverage network extends to your student health services providers.

You may have existing coverage from your college/university. You may be automatically enrolled (read: pay for it) if you don't opt out and provide proof of other insurance.

If you are financially independent—no one can claim you as a dependent on your taxes—then you may qualify for Medicaid. There is nothing wrong with Medicaid, you will receive the same care as someone who is on private insurance. If you aren't eligible for Medicaid, you'll be able to buy insurance from the Affordable Healthcare Act Marketplace at very low cost.

Be wary of any insurance that has limited prescription drug benefits, caps on coverage, and high deductibles. This catastrophic insurance is designed to only help you in case of a terrible health emergency or diagnosis, but catastrophic health insurance can be its own disaster.

What Student Health Services Offer

The most frequent use of student health services is primary care for acute conditions: the flu, strep throat, etc. Most colleges & universities offer much more. Your student health services may offer some or all of the following:

- Gynecological Services
- Allergy Treatment
- Pharmacy
- Labs/Radiology
- Nutrition
- Physical Therapy & Sports Medicine
- Psychiatry
- Travel (vaccines & such)
- Health Promotion

At larger universities with medical schools, student health services operate out of the University Hospital and affiliated practices. Smaller colleges often enter into reciprocity agreements with private practices and local hospitals to provide low or no co-pay services to students. Hours of operation and convenience vary quite a bit. Make sure you keep any appointment you make; a short notice cancellation or no-show typically incurs a fee.

Overall, the process is very similar than going to any healthcare provider. Bring your ID, Student ID, and health insurance card. Show up 15 minutes before your appointment to fill out any necessary paperwork.

Outside the Exam Room

Since each institution is responsible for designing and implementing their programs, the offerings and features vary quite a bit. One reason that the US lags behind other developed nations in longevity and health outcomes is our medical services are geared towards fixing problems instead of preventing them. A habit of using preventative medicine and early intervention is a wonderful example of the long-term thinking that I hope you develop in college (if you don't have it already). Here are some of the most common wellness programs available at colleges & universities.

Diet – Dining halls usually have their menus available online, and you can use these for pre-meal planning (as recommended in the chapter on *Eating, Sleeping, & Exercise*). More robust versions of nutrition planning assistance include connectivity with apps and websites, like mindful.com.

It's common for colleges to offer nutrition counseling and services for students. If you are diabetic, have food allergies, or want to make a life change, avail yourselves of these. It's easy, free and it can make a huge difference in your quality of life.

Exercise – Aside from offering courses, classes, and (often amazing) facilities, colleges offer intramural sports, individual sports, outdoor sports clubs, indoor sports clubs, fitness competitions, exercise clubs, dance studios, organized walks, hikes, and trips. Student health facilities routinely offer blood pressure, cholesterol, and other screenings as well as BMI indexing and personalized fitness programs.

Most schools offer a fitness orientation – If you've never darkened the door of a gym in your life, it can be an intimidating place. Everyone seems to know what to do and how to work the machines without looking like a complete goofball. Sign up for a personal or group fitness orientation, which will give you enough knowledge to get you started. Some colleges are beginning to reward gym attendance with "miles" or "points" that can be redeemed for rewards like towels and sweatshirts.

Health Coaching – Colleges/universities often offer health coaching. This varies from an assessment including your physical fitness level, diet, and exercise habits to an ongoing relationship throughout your freshman year and beyond. These programs are optional, but I highly encourage you to sign up for them.

After Hours Hotline – Many colleges offer after hour hotlines for students in crisis. If your college has one, and you need help, please use it. It's confidential. If your college does not offer a hotline, please check out the chapter on *Mental Health*, where I've listed several.

Stress Management – Colleges take a lot of approaches to stress management. You may have therapy dogs on campus during finals week, drop-in counseling, special courses (in person or online) for managing stress and anxiety, mindfulness/meditation courses, support groups, and other esoteric options. For more on stress and mental health, check out the next chapter, *Mental Health*.

Vaccines – I won't debate vaccines. You should get them. In fact, make sure that you're up on your TDAP, you've had your Meningitis and HPV. College students are at high risk for both Meningitis and HPV. Meningitis often leads to lifelong cognitive impairment and can be fatal. HPV doesn't just cause genital warts, it's also a cause of cervical and anal cancer. Also, get a flu shot every year.

Birth Control – Most colleges provide free condoms. Plan B emergency contraception is typically available as is traditional birth control (pill form, injection, and implants).

Alcohol/Drug Education – The beginning of freshman year is filled with alcohol and drug education. Binge drinking is ubiquitous on college campuses and can be very dangerous. Drug use carries its own risks. A bad decision can radically change your life or even end it. One thing colleges are beginning to discuss, but don't discuss enough, is substance abuse disorders.

If you think you have a substance abuse problem, contact your student health services. The earlier you intervene, the better, but it is *never too late*. Colleges provide resources and assistance to students who are struggling with addiction. This can take the form of counseling, support groups, psychiatric/medical intervention, and access to suboxone and methadone clinics.

Tobacco Cessation – There are a wide variety of support groups and medical intervention services dedicated to helping you quit smoking or using smokeless tobacco. Some student health centers even provide nicotine gum or patches at low or no cost.

Sexual Assault Prevention & Resources – You'll spend a lot of time learning about sexual assault prevention and resources once you get to campus. Sexual assault occurs on college campuses with tragic frequency.

At least 11% of college students are sexually assaulted (the number is probably much higher). Men are also victims of sexual assault.

If you know someone who has been assaulted, or you have been assaulted, contact your student health services immediately. If it's after hours, go to an emergency room or contact the after-hours hotline for your student health services. Your first priority is to take care of yourself. Seek medical care immediately—even if it's just someone to talk to. In the resources section of this chapter, I've listed some hotlines and excellent web based resources.

Resources

End Rape on Campus Hotline & Help	Endrapeoncampus.org
Rainn (sexual assault) Hotline & Help	Rainn.org
Addiction on Campus Alcohol & Drugs	learnpsychology.org/college-campus-addiction-resources/
Health Insurance Healthcare.gov	healthcare.gov/blog/student-health-insurance-options/

28 TAKE CARE OF YOUR MENTAL HEALTH

College is a great experience, but it's not always great. Some parts of college can be difficult or outright suck. **It is not a badge of honor to endure misery nor is it weakness to ask for help.**

College is radically different than it was 20 years ago. Social media has changed the social dynamic, tuition is ridiculous, students are taking longer to graduate, and it's harder to find a good job after college. There is also pressure, particularly on female students, to be effortlessly perfect. Not only are you figuring out how to be an adult, but the most stressful parts of adulthood are dropped on you: money and uncertainty about the future.

Over 50% of students who drop out of college do so for mental health reasons. 73% of students experience a mental health crisis during college. 80% of college students reported feeling overwhelmed within the last year, and 45% of students had felt as if things were hopeless. Over 30% of students have dealt with depression that impairs their ability to function, 57% of women and 40% of men reported feeling overwhelming anxiety in the last year, and 25% of students have contemplated suicide. Suicide is the second leading cause of death for college students.

These are grim statistics, but I want you to look at them from another perspective. **If you're having a tough time, you are far from alone.** Think about it next time you're in class; play the old "look to your left, look to your right game" it's highly likely one of those people is dealing with or has dealt with a mental health issue.

I live with Bipolar II Disorder. My mood disorder became evident in college, but I didn't seek treatment until many years later. I regret not having gotten help earlier, as my disorder had a serious impact on my life, my health, and my relationships. I hope the same does not happen to you.

The State of Mental Health Services on Campus

Colleges are offering more mental health services than ever before, but only 25% of students who could benefit from services take advantage. While the stigma surrounding psychological problems has lessened, it still exists, and a lack of education contributes to students not seeking help. In 2013, 50% of students reported having no education on mental health before college. The lack of mental health education is problematic: many students may ignore or misunderstand symptoms of a mental health problem. I go through symptoms of common mental health issues later this chapter.

Colleges are also increasingly able to help students who have significant mental disorders. With the advent of modern treatment, it is now possible for students with schizophrenia, bipolar, and other serious psychological disorders to attend and complete college.

Crisis

If you're having a crisis, **don't isolate yourself.** Remember, you're going to be OK. Life is long and full of ups and downs, and you will get through this. You can reach out to a friend, family, or a crisis hotline. **You don't have to be suicidal to be in crisis.** No one will ever tell you that your issue isn't serious to call their hotline, and everything is kept confidential. **Your college/university may have one set up as well.**

Sexual Assault Hotline: 1-800-656-HOPE (8255)
Sexual Assault & Abuse   **OR: Chat @** www.rainn.org/online

The JED Foundation: **1-800-273-TALK (8255)**
Emotional Health & **OR: Text "START" to 741-741**
Suicide Prevention **www.JEDFoundation.org**

The Trevor Project: **1-866-488-7386**
LGBTQ **OR: Text 1-202-304-1200**
Text available from 3 pm– 10 pm EST on weekdays and Noon to 7pm EST on weekends.
OR: Chat @ www.thetrevorproject.org

Veterans Crisis Line **1-800-273-8255 (press 1)**
OR: Text 838-255
OR: Chat @ Veteranscrisisline.net

Eating Disorder Hotline	**1-800-931-2237**
	Monday to Thursday 9 am to 9 pm & Friday 9 am to 5 pm.

SAMHSA	**1-800-662-HELP (4357)**
Substance Abuse	

I'm Not Sure if I Need Help

If you're thinking about whether or not you need help, go ahead and schedule an appointment. Do it right away as you may have to wait for an appointment. Alternatively, drop in if the counseling center has walk-in hours. Here are some common reasons why people won't see a counselor and my response to those objections.

Concerns About Convenience and/or Cost – If your campus counseling center is far away or its hours don't align with your schedule, think about what your priorities are. If you believe (and I hope you do) that how you feel directly affects how you perform, then you owe it to yourself to try counseling. **You're not committing to regular counseling, only trying it out once.** Many students only need to go once to work out a personal issue or get through a stressful spot.

As long as the practice is affiliated with your university, there should be no or little cost to you. Your college may also offer a course which could supplant individual counseling, group sessions, or email-based assistance. If you really can't make your campus center work, your college doesn't provide distance options, or your college is one of the few who do not offer mental health services, use your health insurance. (If you don't have health insurance, get it. See the previous chapter). You can also try online counseling for free or a very reasonable price.

Concerns about Privacy – Confidentiality is a big deal in medicine, and it's an even bigger deal for mental health professionals. Breaches of privacy will result in termination of staff or the counselor. The counselor may also lose his/her license and be subject to litigation. Even if the counselor turns out to be your parent's neighbor, he/she will keep your status as a patient and what you discuss confidential.

Concerns about Others – You're under no obligation to tell anyone else that you're in therapy, including your mother, boyfriend/girlfriend, or your roommate. Worried that someone will spot you there? It's exceedingly unlikely, but if you're there, then they are there too. Frankly, you could always lie about it. But, hey, own up to it (if you feel comfortable). There's nothing wrong with needing help.

It Won't Help – When we're in a crisis or have a mental health issue, rational thinking goes out the window. There are two rationales behind "it won't help": my situation is hopeless, and therapy won't work on me. **Both of those reasons are the product of irrational thinking; you are too close to your problems to see them clearly.** Hence, you need an impartial person to give you advice.

Weakness – Everyone has problems. If your car breaks down, you take it to a mechanic. You don't tell your car that it needs to be "tougher" or "cope." Sometimes you need an objective third party, a trained professional, to help you change your perspective or work through a difficult problem. My father, a small businessman, always said, "do what you do and hire out the rest." In my own business, I teach and write. I don't do the accounting or business law. By the same reasoning, I use my therapist and psychiatrist to help me manage my Bipolar II. Seeking help is far braver than pretending nothing is wrong.

Stress

College can be an incredibly stressful time between money, classes, worrying about your future, intimate relationships, friendships, roommates, and generally figuring out life. In the preceding chapter, I talk a lot about how a healthy and balanced life will make you happier (less stressed), and I urge you to check it out. Please don't ignore self-care.

It's normal to feel stressed sometimes. But stress shouldn't be your constant companion, and please don't normalize it. If you're feeling like your stress level it out of control and impacting your life in other ways, please see a counselor. In addition to self-care, organization, time management, and proper goal setting, you can also employ stress-reducing strategies:

Be Careful of Stimulants – Only take drugs that are prescribed to you. Prescription stimulants (Adderall, Ritalin, Dexedrine, Concerta, etc.) are great drugs for those who have a medical condition which warrants their prescription, but these drugs are heavily abused. These can have very serious and dangerous side effects, but stimulant abuse also causes or worsens anxiety and increases your stress level. Caffeine is a stimulant too, and, as much as I love caffeine, it's not always the answer. Like any stimulant, caffeine can make you more anxious and feel more frantic and stressed.

Meditate – Studies have demonstrated the effectiveness of meditation for reducing stress and increasing positive feelings in college students. Some colleges have started meditation courses or programs, but you can also find meditation apps and online guides.

Hobby – It's great to pursue a hobby, something that's not for your resume. Make that time and you'll find it's associated with a reduction in stress and anxiety and an increase in positive feelings. Check out the chapter on *Getting Involved* for some ideas.

Breathe – If you have a wearable, it's got a relaxation breathing routine on it. I suggest using it. If you don't have a FitBit, Apple watch, or the like, you can do it on your own. There are a ton of different breathing exercises out there, I like the 4-7-8 method. The key is to breathe with your stomach, so keep a hand on your chest and on your belly, the belly should inflate and the chest shouldn't rise. You take a deep breath in for four seconds; hold it for seven seconds; and then exhale for 8 seconds. Repeat until you feel calm. If this one doesn't suit your fancy, a quick google search will give you dozens to try.

Anxiety

Anxiety is the most common reason students seek help from college counseling centers. In 2013, over 46% of students who went to counseling did so for anxiety. Anxiety is a broad term and includes things like panic attacks (acute anxiety), general anxiety (chronic anxiety), and situational anxiety (social anxiety and test anxiety, for example). Because it's a broad category, anxiety manifests in many ways, and you may not even recognize the symptoms as a product of anxiety.

Everyone gets anxious; it's part of the human condition. But if anxiety interferes with your life or impairs your ability to function, please address it. Below are some indicators that may indicate your anxiety is more than usual. You don't need to have all of these symptoms or you may have symptoms that aren't listed.

- Constant and unsubstantiated worry that causes significant distress and interferes with daily life.

- Avoiding social situations for fear of being judged, embarrassed, or humiliated.
- Panic attacks where you can't determine a cause and preoccupation with the fear of having another panic attack.
- Recurring nightmares, flashbacks, or emotional numbing related to a traumatic event that occurred several months or years before.[2]

Anxiety disorders are very common: approximately 12% of college students live with an anxiety disorder.

Depression

College students experience depression at a much higher rate than the general population. Commonly cited explanations are the increase of screen use and distortion of expectation and peers caused by social media. **Between 7 and 9% of students are depressed or have been clinically depressed. A far higher percentage of students report feeling depressed or very depressed within the last year.**

It can be hard to self-identify symptoms of depression, and, if you're relatively new to college, your friends may not pick up on it as well. Your college friends probably don't know you as well and won't be as likely to pick up on you acting differently. (Remember that if you're feeling low and it seems like no one notices). Here are some symptoms of depression:

- Feelings of sadness, tearfulness, emptiness, or hopelessness
- Small matters make you irritable, frustrated, or cause you to have outbursts.
- Agitation, anxiety, or restlessness
- Loss of interest or pleasure in activities like hobbies, sports, or time with friends
- Change in appetite & eating habits, this may result in weight loss or weight gain
- Slowed thinking, speaking, or movement
- Trouble thinking, concentrating, making decisions, or remembering important details
- Feelings of worthlessness or guilt, a fixation on past failures, or blaming yourself for things outside of your control

---

[2] Anxiety & Depression Association of America: adaa.org

- Frequent or recurring thoughts of death, suicidal thoughts, or suicide attempts
- Unexplained physical problems, typically aches and pains[3]

ADHD

Modern ADHD treatment has allowed students with ADHD to attend college and thrive. While it's likely you would be diagnosed before college, for some, ADHD may go undiagnosed until they're in the more challenging, self-structured environment of college. Don't jump to assumptions if you haven't been diagnosed but think you may be ADHD. College students often misdiagnose themselves with ADHD. As a disorder, ADHD has three primary types:

Inattentive – Is the form of ADHD that is most likely to go undiagnosed. Women are more likely to have this form of ADHD, but it occurs in men as well. The behaviors are harder to peg as ADHD symptoms; people with inattentive ADHD tend to be spacey, disorganized, and may seem apathetic to outsiders (versus hyperactive and impulsive behaviors). Here are some symptoms of inattentive ADHD:

- Often makes careless mistakes
- Difficulty sustaining attention
- Frequently has to ask people to repeat themselves or is accused of not listening when spoken to
- Difficulty organizing tasks and activities
- Difficulty following through on instructions and finishing projects
- Dislike of or reluctant to engage in tasks requiring sustained mental effort
- Often loses things, particularly items necessary for tasks or activities
- Forgetful in daily activities
- Is often easily distracted by extraneous stimuli

---

[3] The Mayo Clinic: www.mayoclinic.org

Hyperactive-Impulsive – This fits your stereotype of ADHD, an overly energetic person. Symptoms of hyperactive-impulsive ADHD include

- Fidgets with hands or feet or squirms in seat
- Leaves seat in classroom or situations where remaining seated is expected.
- Runs about or climbs excessively in situations in which it is inappropriate *or* you have a persistent feeling of restlessness
- Acting, or feeling as though, you are "driven by a motor"
- Excessive talking
- Impulse to blurt out answers before the questions have been completed.
- Difficulty waiting in line or waiting your turn in a group setting
- Interrupts or intrudes on others[4]

Combined Type – ADHD occurs when someone has symptoms of both Hyperactive-Impulsive & Inattentive.

ADHD affects more than grades. Students with poorly managed ADHD are at much higher risk for car accidents, sexually transmitted infections, unplanned pregnancy, eating disorders, alcohol/drug abuse, and issues with social adjustment.

25 – 50% of ADHD college students suffer from depression or anxiety issues, and eating disorders are four times more likely in women with ADHD.

ADHD requires management. **Do not stop taking your medicine when you start college.** Make sure you continue treatment by making a plan to before you arrive on campus (or as soon as you can). If you think you have ADHD and it has gone undiagnosed, your college will likely have the ability to test you or can refer you for testing at low or no cost. Please check out the chapter on *Accommodations for Disability* for how your college can help you.

PTSD

Over 50% of men and 50% of women experience at least one traumatic event in their lifetime. Approximately 8% of those men and 20% of those women will develop PTSD. PTSD is not limited to veterans (for more specific veterans information, see the chapter on *Veterans*). A history of abuse, violence, sexual assault, serious accidents, loss, and disasters can all be inciting

---

[4] Additude Magazine: www.additudemag.com

incidents. In fact, college students have a higher incidence of PTSD than the general population. Symptoms of PTSD include

- Recurring thoughts of the event
- Flashbacks/Nightmares
- Emotional Numbness or apathy
- Intense guilt or worry/anxiety
- Angry outbursts or irritability
- Feeling hyper-alert (on edge)
- Avoiding thoughts or situations that are reminiscent of the trauma.

Depression is incredibly common among students with PTSD. Substance abuse and dependence, anxiety problems, self-harm, suicidal thoughts and attempts, and eating disorders occur more frequently in students with PTSD.

Eating Disorders

You're likely familiar with anorexia, bulimia, and, binge eating disorder. Those are severe, life-threatening conditions. College students—including men—are most at risk of developing an eating disorder. It's estimated that between 10 and 20% of women and 4 to 10% of men suffer from an eating disorder. Eating disorders exist on a continuum, and you can have a problem with eating without having an eating disorder.

Disordered Eating – Disordered eating manifests in many ways: preoccupation with fad diets or cleanses; over-exercising; abusing laxatives; binging/purging; preoccupation with "cleanses" (cleanses don't work, that's not me saying that, that's science); or restricting fats, dairy or gluten without a *valid* medical reason. An intentionally chosen "diet" can devolve into unhealthy dieting, and it does about 35% of the time. Of those disordered eating cases, 20 – 25% develop eating disorders.

Eating Disorders – The difference between "disordered eating" and an eating disorder is when the behavior is sustained over time and has begun to dominate other areas of life. Eating disorders are life threatening medical conditions.

Anorexia – The hallmark of anorexia is a distorted body image, and untreated anorexia is almost always fatal. Anorexics go to extremes to avoid eating, and they may exercise obsessively.

Physical Symptoms	Other Symptoms
Thinning Hair	Intense Drive for Thinness
Dry, Flaking Skin	Fears of Becoming Fat
Lack of Menstruation	Denying Hunger
Weight Less than 85% of Ideal	Avoiding Food
	Obsession with Dieting
	Social Withdrawal
	Emotional Changes

Bulimia – Bulimia is typically characterized by binge and purge cycles where large amounts of food are consumed in a short amount of time, and then vomiting is forced. But other methods may be used to compensate for binging, including excessive exercise, laxatives, and diet pills. **Bulimia is often unrecognized because most bulimics maintain a healthy weight**. The costs on the body, however, are terrible and can be fatal.

Physical Symptoms

- Broken Blood Vessels Around Eyes
- Stained/deteriorating teeth
- Stomach Pain
- Weakness/Fatigue
- Lack of Menstruation

Other Symptoms

- Eating Large quantities of food with no weight change.
- Smell of vomit
- Trips to the bathroom after meals
- Excessive use of diuretics
- Eating while others sleep
- Excessive exercise
- Distorted Body Image

Binge Eating Disorder – Individuals with binge eating disorder typically binge (like in bulimia), but they do not purge. The two are not exclusive; many who have bulimia also have binge eating disorder. Binge eaters feel a lack of control over their behavior. Unlike bulimia or anorexia, students with binge eating disorder tend to be overweight.

<u>Symptoms</u>

- Eating in Secret
- Eating when not hungry
- Eating to cope with stress or negative moods
- Unable to control the amount eaten[5]

Men and Eating Disorders – More and more men are developing eating disorders. Statistically, gay males have the highest risk, and male eating disorders are often centered on an obsession with exercise (I discuss exercise addiction in the chapter *Eat, Sleep, & Exercise*). Males have a higher risk of dying from eating disorders, in part because of the stigma of eating disorders being a "female condition".

Substance Abuse

I'm also not going to go over the dangers of binge drinking; it is dangerous, and it can have disastrous consequences. I'm also not going to go over the dangers of illegal drugs; they can be dangerous (particularly opiates) and there can be serious consequences.

Instead, I want to focus on something many colleges under-educate on, substance abuse disorders and their warning signs. You may think you'll stop any bad habits or risky behavior as soon as your handed your diploma. You may be right, but you may be wrong. The costs and consequences of being wrong aren't worth paying. If you use substances, do so safely and responsibly. Almost 23% of college students meet the diagnostic criteria for substance abuse disorder. These warning signs are true for alcohol, marijuana, hallucinogens, inhalants, opioids, sedatives (Ambien, Xanax, etc.), cocaine, methamphetamine, Adderall and other stimulant ADHD drugs.

---

[5] Symptoms for all eating disorders from the Walden Center: www.waldencenter.org

Symptoms of Substance Abuse Disorders

1. **Inability to control how long you use for or how much you use.** Essentially, if you have it, you take it.

2. **Wanting to cut back or stop but being unable to do so.** If you've made plans to cut back or stop, but then broken those plans/promises despite your best effort, this applies to you.

3. **You spend a large percentage of your time planning to get the drug, using the drug, or recovering from the drug.**

4. **Cravings so intense you have a hard time thinking about anything else.**

5. **Significant damage to relationships, your studies, or negative consequences.** For example, you miss deadlines, repeatedly miss class, have problems with roommates, friends, family members, or classmates because of your substance abuse. You have stopped activities that are important to you, and you're not meeting your responsibilities.

6. **Risky use** includes ignoring warning signs or health problems related to or made worse by use. Some behaviors, such as snorting prescription pills and IV drug use, are inherently risky.

7. **Increased tolerance or withdrawal** are indicators that your body is habituating to the frequent use of a drug.

If You Think You Have a Substance Abuse Problem

Don't wait to address it. It will only get worse. You'll hurt more, psychologically, and it'll be harder.

Except for some conservative Christian colleges, schools will not punish you for seeking help. Your college may be well-equipped to help you. Some schools, notably Rutgers and Texas Tech, provide sober housing as well as support groups and access to 12-step and other recovery meetings. Other colleges have counseling centers that are well equipped to help you or refer you to the appropriate in or outpatient clinic.

If you think you need help, you need help. Don't go it alone. You can try out 12-step meetings, SMART Recovery, private counseling, and/or online counseling.

For many of you, abstinence is not the only option. You can try programs for moderating your drinking or substance use (see the *Resources* section of this chapter). If those don't work, and you cannot control your intake, don't despair, but take action. I promise you, if you don't your life will fall apart, or you may die.

Self-Harm

26% of students who have used on-campus counseling services have reported intentionally injuring themselves. If you have hurt yourself, or are considering hurting yourself, please don't feel alone. Don't feel ashamed, either. You're hurting and you need help. Call a hotline. If you're not in crisis, set an appointment with your school's counseling center or another mental health professional. Above all, don't isolate yourself. Take care of yourself. Everything else can wait.

If You are Entering College with a Diagnosis

If you've been diagnosed with a condition that will continue into college, make a care plan for yourself. If you're going to school away from home, this is even more important. I also strongly encourage you to inform your college/university, particularly if your diagnosis can impact you academically. Even if it can't, your school may be able to provide extra support. It's better to have accommodations or extra support and not need it than to need it and not have it. Please read the next chapter on *Accommodations for Disability*.

Where Else to Look for Help

Many campus counseling centers are overwhelmed and may not be able to help you immediately (unless you're in crisis). Here are some other options.

On-Campus – Aside from any psychiatric and counseling services offered by the University, your college may have support groups for students living with or recovering from mental health conditions and substance abuse disorders.

Online Counseling – Online counseling has exploded in popularity. You can find a number of options that are low cost and many take insurance.

Online Support Groups – If you have a specific issue, a support group can be a wonderful augment to any treatment you receive.

Off-Campus – Most mental health professionals with offices near college campuses have extensive experience working with students. Ask for a referral from your campus center if you can.

Eat, Sleep, Exercise – Self-care is so important. Try it.

<u>Resources</u>

ADHD Resources ADDA	add.org/college-students/
Depression Toolkit University of Michigan	depressiontoolkit.org/lifespan/college.asp
Addiction on Campus Alcohol & Drugs	learnpsychology.org/college-campus-addiction-resources/
Anxiety Disorders ADAA	adaa.org/living-with-anxiety/college-students
Eating Disorders Assessment & Resources	nationaleatingdisorders.org

29 ACCOMMODATIONS FOR DISABILITY

All colleges and postsecondary educational programs are required to provide accommodations to students who have disabilities. Statistics indicate that approximately 11% of undergraduate students have a disability. The majority of those disabilities are related to learning. I feel that is well below the true number, as it doesn't account for the underreporting of emotional and learning disabilities.

In spirit, colleges are friendly to those with physical, learning, and emotional disabilities. In practice, however, colleges are often slow to respond when it comes to creating new accommodations.

Applying for accommodations as early as possible—even when you don't think you'll need them—is vital to your success. I cannot stress this enough.

Your Rights
1. You cannot be asked to disclose if you have a disability
2. You cannot be denied admission based on your disability
3. You cannot be excluded from any program, class, or activity
4. Your disability will remain confidential.

There is a bit of a caveat, although it's <u>very</u> unlikely to affect you. Colleges aren't required to make accommodations that would compromise the program or academic integrity of a course.

Your Responsibilities

Unlike high school, the burden is on you.

1. You have to go to the college/university and identify yourself as disabled.

2. You have to provide appropriate up-to-date documentation, the definition of up-to-date and appropriate depend on the disability and the college.

3. You have to request accommodations that make the playing field even. You have discretion over what accommodations you request, and you also have control over which accommodations you use.

4. You have to identify as a person with disabilities to each professor and provide a copy of the individualized student profile developed with the college's disability service office.

5. You are responsible for your education.

6. You may need to remind your professors of your accommodations before big tests and assignments (this avoids awkwardness or miscommunication).

Why People Don't Seek Accommodations & Why That's Foolish

1. **Stigma/Lack of Opportunity** – The fear of being judged is the number one reason students fail to disclose their disability and request accommodations. But, privacy is the number one rule. The disability office operates under many of the same rules that govern a doctor's office or mental health practice. You can be confident, even at a small school or in a rural setting, that the staff will work hard to preserve your privacy.

   Similarly, professors are required to preserve your privacy as much as possible. If you've gotten accommodations and are unsure of how to approach your professor, **go to office hours**. I think these conversations are best held in person in private; remember to bring your documentation from the disability office.

2. **They Don't Believe They Will Receive Accommodations –** Students feel that their diagnosis won't result in accommodations. This is particularly common with processing disorders and mental health issues. <u>You don't know what the school will do</u>. The worst thing they can do is say no, which you can appeal. A much more likely scenario is that you will receive some accommodations and be directed to additional resources that can support your success in college.

3. **They Don't Believe Their Diagnosis Impacts Academic Performance –** Students feel that their diagnosis doesn't impact their studies. It may not, but it's almost impossible to know—<u>particularly before your semester starts</u>. Things may change, your classes may be tougher than you expect, you may experience some personal difficulty, or you may have other issues with managing your condition. **It's not about how well you do, it's about how well you could do.**

Get the process started. You don't have a crystal ball. You don't know what's going to happen, and it's better to be safe than sorry.

<u>Learning and Emotional Disabilities</u>

A depressive episode made it impossible for me to go to classes and I did not get help until it was too late…I was withdrawn and I could never afford to go back because I lost my scholarship….[6]

The student quoted above is, unfortunately, far from alone. College students are unaware of how to get accommodations, wait to long to begin the process, or (most commonly) are afraid to seek accommodations. **Students with emotional disabilities can receive accommodations.** Over 45% of students who dropped out of college because of mental health reasons were not receiving accommodations or accessing mental health services.

Without support, emotional and learning difficulties often end college careers. It's common that students lose their scholarships or financial aid due to low GPA, lack of progress (not enough credits earned), or dropping below full-time status.

---

[6] National Alliance of Mental Health Survey Respondent: *College Students Speak: A survey Report on Mental   Health.*

Emotional & Learning Disabilities that are Given Accommodations

This is not a comprehensive list. Don't be disheartened If you don't see your diagnosis on here.

Learning Disabilities
- ADHD
- Dyslexia
- Dysgraphia
- Dyscalculia
- Processing Disorders
- Autism
- Traumatic Brain Injury*

Emotional Disabilities
- Depression
- Anxiety Disorders
- Bipolar Disorder
- Clyclothymia
- Schizophrenia
- Eating Disorders
- PTSD#
- Drug Abuse/Addiction
- OCD
- Sleep Disorders

Getting Accommodations

The only difference between a new and existing diagnosis is that a new diagnosis may require additional testing or other medical verification.

Step 1: Contact the disabilities office and begin the paperwork to register as a student with a disability. In your initial conversation, ask what documentation you'll need. <u>Contact them as soon as possible</u>.

Step 2: Collect the required documentation. Colleges have different criteria, but learning disabilities typically require testing. As long as you were tested fairly recently, you should be ok. You may, however, need new or additional testing (more on this below). The testing needs to be fairly recent. If you're a recent or new high school grad, a 504 or IEP plan showing accommodations received in high school is something you'll want/need to have.

---

* Traumatic Brain injury is not limited to veterans. Students who played contact sports (particularly football and soccer), been in a serious accident, and students who had had one or more concussions may have some form of TBI.

\# PTSD is not limited to veterans either. Trauma comes in many forms.

Step3: Meet with the disabilities coordinator/staff member. <u>Bring your documentation</u>. This is an opportunity for you to say what accommodations worked for you in the past and what you think would be helpful in college (know *why* you want something), even if the accommodation isn't on your   high   school   504/IEP. Remember, it's better to ask for more than you think you need, as you can choose which accommodations you use.

Step 4: Receive decision. If it's not in your favor, you can appeal the decision.

Step 5: Give accommodations letter to professor and have a discussion about how your accommodations will work in the context of their course.

Step 6: Things may change and you may need to ask for additional accommodations. <u>If your accommodations aren't working, seek assistance right away</u>.

Accommodations Requested (Learning/Emotional Disabilities)

Extended Time – You can have extra time to complete exams. Most commonly, students are granted 1.5 times the regular length of the examination. For example, you'd get 90 minutes for a 60-minute exam.

Separate Testing – You can request to have your test taken in another quiet location.

Altered Tests – The format of the test can be changed. For example, you may have someone read questions to you or record your answers.

Materials Format – You can request audiobooks (instead of textbooks) and the like.

Priority Registration – If your disability affects access or requires that you keep a particular schedule, you may qualify for priority registration. This is also true if you would benefit from smaller class sizes. This is a very important and often overlooked accommodation.

Anonymous Note-taker – You can have a note-taker in class to help you. The note- taker doesn't have to sit next to you, nor will anyone know you have a note-taker.

Written Instructions – If you have difficulty processing verbal instructions, you can request that all course instructions be written out and given to you electronically or in print.

Permission to Record Lectures – You can audio or video record lectures. You may also have access to college/university owned recording equipment.

Reduced Course Load – Generally, colleges require full time students to take 12 hours per semester (or equivalent thereof). You may be able to keep your scholarships and financial aid by taking fewer courses. This is a very important and often overlooked accommodation.

Course Substitutions – You may be able to substitute a required course. This is more common in physical disabilities.

I Need New/More Testing

At larger schools, particularly those with medical schools, you can receive psychiatric services and psychological testing. Small schools may or may not have those services. In those cases, life will be easier if you have good health insurance. You'll have a more consistent level of care, and you'll find it easier to get the services you need. Check out the chapter on *Student Health Services* for more on health insurance.

Some testing may not be covered by insurance. Generally this happens if you have already been diagnosed. In many states, insurance appeals have a high likelihood of success. There may be local foundations and non-profit mental health agencies that can secure you free or low-cost testing. Talk to your disabilities office, and if they don't have any ready solutions (they may or may not) look around online, or call a mental health hotline (not a crisis line).

Regardless, **getting your accommodations in place needs to be a spending priority**. If you have no other options, I recommend that you borrow additional student loans to cover the cost of any testing necessary.

Physical Disabilities

Often, physical disabilities come with mobility issues and a need for convenient specialist care. If you have mobility issues and I'm catching you while you're still applying for schools, you'll want to do a very thorough tour of the campus to realize how "accessible" the campus and the dorms really are for your needs.

Physical disabilities include permanent disabilities, temporary disabilities, as well as chronic health conditions. The list below is by no means complete; it's only meant to show the breadth of physical disabilities. **Always remember, not all disabilities are visible.**

<u>Examples of Physical Disabilities</u>

Low Vision/Blindness	Mobility Issues
Cancer	Epilepsy
Diabetes	Chronic Fatigue Syndrome
HIV/AIDS	Renal Disease
Chemical Sensitivities	Muscular Dystrophy
Multiple Sclerosis	

Accommodations for Physical Disabilities

Here a partial list of accommodations for physical disabilities and chronic health conditions.

Recorder or Note Take	Accessible Seating
Accessible Bathrooms	Scribes for Quizzes/Exams
Additional Time	Separate Testing
Relaxation of Attendance Policies	Relocation of Classroom or
Prearranged or Frequent Breaks	Lab to Accessible Facility
Modified Courses	Use of Computer Software
Reading or Test Taking	Preferential Seating
Accessible Lab Equipment	Large Print or Braille
(Computer & Science Labs)	Raised Line Drawings /
Descriptions of Visual Aids	Tactile Models

Getting Accommodations for Physical Disabilities

The process for receiving accommodations for physical disabilities and chronic health conditions is roughly the same as for emotional and learning disabilities, but the process is usually a little smoother and easier.

Step 1: Contact the disabilities office and begin the paperwork to register as a student with a disability. In your initial contact, ask what documentation you'll need. Do this as soon as possible.

Step 2: Collect Documentation. Colleges have different criteria but you'll need some sort of medical verification for physical disabilities. Depending on the disability, you may need verification that's somewhat recent. That verification may need to include recommendations for accommodations as well as specifically listing any limitations you have.

Step 3: Meet with the disabilities coordinator/staff member. Bring your documentation. This is an opportunity for you to say what accommodations worked in the past and what you think would be helpful in college (know why you want something), even if the accommodation isn't on your high school 504/IEP or your medical verification. Your physical and learning environment is much different in college, and, as such, you may need different accommodations. Remember, it's better to ask for more accommodations, as you can choose which you want to use.

Step 4: Receive decision. Remember, you can appeal the decision.

Step 5: Give accommodations letter to each of your professors and have a discussion about how your accommodations will work in the context of their course.

Step 6: Things may change and you may need to ask for additional accommodations. <u>If your accommodations aren't working, get help right away.</u>

<u>**Resources**</u>

Reasonable Accommodations Jane E. Jarrow, Ph.D.	bucknell.edu/Documents/Accessibility/Yarrow-What-is-a-reasonable-Accommodation.pdf

30 PLAN AND PERSIST

I know I'm repeating myself, but graduating college requires a different skill set and mindset than high school. Graduating high school was, for most of you, a matter up of showing up regularly, doing some work, and not getting kicked out. To be very honest, a high school diploma in the United States is not much more than a certificate of attendance.

Graduating college requires planning, persistence, and it will require you to make tradeoffs.

No One Told Me
I talk to a lot of college students, and I hear, "no one told me" somewhat frequently. Before you think I'm jumping on your generation with some anti-millennial screed, hear me out. You are unaccustomed to having to find your own answers and negotiating complicated and sometimes conflicting systems (like colleges) because you've never done it before.

Life has saved all the confusion of adulthood for adulthood, and you can view college as your first taste of the wonderful world of large employers, mortgage companies, student loan servicers, health insurance, and so on.

College can be a big, confusing mess. If you get lost in that mess, you're the one who pays—not the college. Here's how to manage:

1. **Make Your Own Map –** Understand what it will take for you to graduate in four years. Not just a list of classes, but a list of classes in order, when those classes are available, and what prerequisites you'll need. Your map also needs to include general education requirements. You should have other maps for career or graduate school goals.

2. **A Fragile Plan is No Plan at All** – If there's only one way forward, your plan is fragile. If your plan is that fragile, it's a wish, not a plan. One of two things is happening: you aren't seeing all the ways you can get to your objective (see number 4) or your goal is overly specific and probably too far outside of your control (see the chapter *Set Goals*).

3. **Trust but Verify** – Advisers are great, older friends are great, classmates are great, but fact check everything from career advice to courses. Never take anyone's word on what you can or cannot do as definitive, particularly if that word is "no".

4. **The Way is Broad** – We often think there's only one way to reach a destination. We confuse the most popular route with the only route. If you're changing majors, transferring schools, or deciding to give up on something, look around, ask around, and research other routes to get to where you want to be.

5. **Big Decisions Require Big Reasons** – Changing majors, deciding to give up on a career/graduate/professional school plans, or transferring schools should not be an emotional decision. You have to weigh the benefits and the consequences of that action.

Persist

Even if you stay committed to the same goal, your plan will change. A Prussian gentleman said a battle plan, "never survives first contact with the enemy." He was right, and while—hopefully—your college career does not have the characteristics of a war, things will change.

Bad things will happen, good things will happen, the school will change its offerings or requirements. What you need for your particular goal may change. A robust plan is the first step to reaching your goal, but it's only a start.

You have to be able to connect with your goal even when it feels like a wall has gone up between you and it. As someone who writes books, I can tell you that the goal of having written a book seems terrifically close sometimes (even when it's tens of thousands of words away). Sometimes that goal seems incredibly remote, and I wonder if its worth all the effort. What if no one buys it? What if I get bad reviews? What if they think I'm dumb for trying?

Everyone feels like this from time-to-time. Here's what I tell myself, and hopefully it will help you.

My goals are for me, not you. It's easy to think that others are very invested in our success or failure. They aren't, except your parents, close friends, significant other, and children. When I work on a book, It's an extension of who I am and who I want to be. Yes, I want to sell books and yes I want good reviews (please consider leaving one), but the project is personally important to me. It has a significance that's separate from the business side of publishing. **Whenever things get tough, remember why you started.**

Tough things are the most valuable. I learn and grow the most when things are hard. I think "tough" implicitly includes the possibility of failure or quitting. Tough implies you choose to be there and you choose to stick it out.

Quitting now doesn't make sense. It would be silly of me to quit halfway through a book, after I've already spent several hundred hours researching and writing. It's possible that I'll decide to quit writing books after this one. I doubt it, but it is something I'll take the time to think about. Even if I expect that I won't quit, actively choosing not to quit marries me more closely to my goal. I don't mind quitting at all, just wait until you're at a natural starting point.

Wait until the semester is over to change majors. Wait until the year is over before you decide to transfer.

I believe I can create my future. Life is full of uncertainty. I could get sick or die. My book could bomb and I could get sued by the for-profit colleges I wasn't very nice about earlier. But I can always write another book, and if I can figure out why this book didn't do well the next one may do great. I could get sued by for-profit colleges, but I have a pretty good lawyer. **I have a specific idea of what I want tomorrow to look like, and my best shot of getting there is making the right choices day-by-day.**

In This Section

General Education Requirements – Are the courses many students dread that provide the underpinning of a liberal arts education. I discuss how these vary by school and go over the most common models and what they may look like at your college.

Majors – Your major is the defining characteristic of your undergraduate degree. I cover choosing a major, the economics of majors, and whether double majoring is worth it.

Changing Majors – The majority of college students change majors. Here's how and when to do it without delaying graduation.

Advising – Your relationship with your adviser is the most important of your undergraduate career.

Resources

Grit: The Power of Passion & Perserverance	Angela Duckworth

31 GENERAL EDUCATION REQUIREMENTS

The Background

In the United States, General Education/Core Curriculum requirements began to appear right before the first World War. The purpose of general education varies by institution but retains the same underlying principles:

1. **Avoid academic specialization** – Colleges and Universities strive to provide an education that is greater than pre-professional or career training.
2. **Provide the cultural foundations necessary for life** – This is sometimes referred to as a moral imperative, for example, "the inculcation of moral values."

But Why?

Believe it or not, general education requirements have a strong civic motivation. Colleges and universities used to be much more involved in the lives of their students (some still are for better or worse). This institutional parenting—referred to as *a parens patriae*—took a keen interest in the moral development of students.

You can blame radicalism and anti-intellectualism for having to take college algebra, economics, English composition, public speaking, or whatever else you may detest. Colleges sought to insulate the US from radical populism (and later fascism) by creating well-rounded students, steeped in the history and philosophy of western civilization. If, instead, your very valid question is "why did I have to read all that, you jerk?" It's because I think the liberal arts ideal and general education requirements are important for you and society.

What do General Education Requirements Entail?

General education requirements vary considerably as each school creates its program. Go to Google and search for your "college/university name general education requirements."

Over 70% of colleges and universities use some form of the distribution method (more on this in the next section), but there are usually additional features. There may be classes you can't bypass (common at schools with a religious affiliation and smaller schools). General education requirements seem more onerous than they are. But when you break it down semester by semester, one course at a time, it's not bad at all.

The What's What of General Education Requirements

Distribution Requirements 76%[7]

Distribution Requirements form the basis for the general education curriculum at the majority of colleges and universities. Think of distribution requirements as the base model of a car, to which other features added. When we think of general education requirements, what we're really thinking of is the Distribution Requirements (or Core Curriculum requirements). Of colleges/universities that use the distribution model, only 8% of schools used distribution only, 24% had at least one other feature, and 68% employed multiple features.

What are distribution requirements? Distribution Requirements lumps departments into big categories. For example, political science, history, and psychology are typically all in the social sciences category. A common format is lumping all disciplines into three categories: social sciences, humanities, and STEM. In it's most basic form, you'll be required to take so many hours out of each basket. Often specific types of courses are required, a lab science, a math course, a composition course, a literature or theater course, an art or music course.

At most schools, many of these hours can be transferred in. For example, AP scores can exempt you from some classes.

---

[7] The percentages are all from a 2015 survey by Inside Higher Ed

Colleges believe that this gives you, the student, more agency. The thinking goes that you'll learn better and be more motivated to explore new ideas and disciplines if you aren't coerced.

Core Curriculum 42%

Core Curriculums are a more restrictive form of a Distribution Requirement system. Students have fewer options and more specific requirements. In elite schools, there has been a general trend of moving *from* Core Curriculums *to* Distribution Requirements. For example, Yale and Harvard both did so in the early 2000's.

Capstone (in majors) 76%

Capstones, like their architectural namesake, are meant to be a culmination. There are two types of capstone experiences, capstones limited to your major and capstones revolving around general education.

Major Capstones take a lot of forms. They usually require long-term research, work/internship experience, and/or the completion of a significant project. The results are presented as a portfolio, presentation, performance, paper, or a film. For example, a political science capstone may be working with a non-profit on interfacing with local government. A social work capstone may involve grant writing or an internship. Engineers may compete in a competition, or attempt to solve a real-world problem.

Capstone (In General Ed) 60%

General Ed Capstones tend to be more holistic. General education capstones involve the study of multiple disciplines with embedded assignments working towards the capstone. The idea is to track the development of skills like writing and critical thinking and demonstrate your ability to be an "active citizen" or "understand the responsibility of global citizenship" or "have ethical and critical sensibility".

Culminating Studies/Experiences 46%

For the most part, Culminating Studies/Experiences are the same as a Capstone, and the terms are used interchangeably. They may be more restrictive. For example, every senior may be required to write an original thesis.

Upper-Level General Ed Requirements 44%

You'll be required to take enough of a discipline (not your major, or courses required by your major) to be able to take upper-division coursework. For most disciplines, this you would take two introductory courses and then a 300 level course (your numbering system may vary). For example, you take (or transfer in) Bio 101 and Bio 102. You could then take a 300 level course—likely without having to take a lab science. By requiring upper division general education credits forces the college forces you to focus on a discipline outside your major, while also preventing grade shopping.

Common Intellectual Experiences 26%

Common Intellectual Experiences are similar to the next entry, Learning Communities. Fundamentally, common intellectual experiences combine broad themes—artificial intelligence, sustainability, etc.—across courses to encourage students to think holistically about major, multidisciplinary issues.

They can involve specific courses, readings, discussion groups, service projects, and trips. Common intellectual experiences can be mandatory, most commonly for first-year students, although they are occasionally required for upper division students as a department requirement. Common Intellectual Experiences may also be elective.

Learning Communities 22%

Generally, a learning community is a group of students who take one or more courses together. Learning communities can be based on academic or career goals, common courses, dorm assignment, peer mentoring/tutoring, and faculty mentoring. Living Learning Communities are discussed in the chapter on *Living in a Dorm*.

Here are some of the more common learning communities:

Linked Courses – students take two connected courses one based on skills (writing, information literacy, etc.) and one informational course (chemistry, history, economics).

Learning Clusters – students take three, or more, courses with a shared theme. These courses will be interdisciplinary (in different departments).

Freshman Interest Groups – students share a major and often receive learning community specific advising.

Federated Learning Communities – students complete a learning cluster, however, a professor teaching one of the courses in the cluster takes the other courses with the students. That professor then teaches an additional "Master Learner" course.

Take the Easy Way Out or Challenge Yourself?

At most colleges, you can make general education requirements as easy or as tough as you like. What do I think you should do? It's a tough call because it's about more than your comfort level.

Students are increasingly motivated by money. They want the best path to the best job, and that's one reason why there are more business majors than ever before. Don't judge them (or yourself) too harshly. It's a rational reaction to the ridiculous cost of tuition. It's a reasonable response to the environment you grew up in, where student debt and poor job prospects kept newly minted graduates mired in underemployment. Students don't want to risk another semester at school, and they know top employers take GPA's seriously.

Students planning on graduate or professional school want to protect their GPA. That makes sense. Be aware, though, that grad school committees will pay attention to what you took *outside* of your major. They would be much more impressed by a course about the literature of the lost generation than a course discussing the philosophy of 1980's action movies.

I believe there is value to pushing yourself in college. I also believe that there is value to the traditional liberal arts education. Most of all, I think college is a time to try out subjects you'd never consider. Life will take you funny places, be willing to expose yourself to the envelope of serendipity. **I suggest that you be a prudent hero: push yourself, but don't become a martyr.** The occasional puff class won't kill you.

32 MAJORS

Your major (or majors) are the defining characteristic of your undergraduate (B.A. or B.S.) degree. If anyone has ever told you, "I got a degree in…." they're telling you what their major was. Your major gives you an undergraduate specialization in a field. It's a set of courses of increasing specificity and complexity that prepare you for a job, further studies in that field, or professional school.

What's in a Major

There's quite a bit of variability in how many credit hours a major requires, anywhere between 30 and 45. In addition to the hours spent *within* the discipline, you will be required to take certain courses outside the discipline. For example, political science majors may have to take intro microeconomics and intro macroeconomics, chemistry majors typically take several calculus courses, and biology majors have to take general and organic chemistry. These courses will usually help satisfy your general education requirements, particularly if your school uses a distribution system. (Check out the previous chapter on *General Education Requirements*).

Bachelor of Art or Science

Many disciplines (psychology, economics, etc.) offer different degree tracks for students which result in either a B.A. Bachelor of Arts or a B.S. Bachelor of Science degrees are usually more specific and technical. For most scientific and technical fields, a Bachelors of Science is the only degree option.

If your discipline offers you a choice between B.A. and B.S., which you get is up to you. Depending on your post-college goals, one may have an advantage. In general, I think that B.S. degrees (when they are an option) are more highly considered, but remember, your college and program may be different.

The Three Types of Majors

I made three broad, overlapping categories to discuss and consider majors. I think you should love your major, but you should always see it as a means to an end. It's a stepping stone. Your career plan and goals are not the same as your major, just because your plan changes doesn't mean your major has to.

1. **Majors leading directly into a professional career**

    Accounting degrees often include enough hours to sit for the CPA, nursing majors have the required clinical hours and knowledge to sit for the NCLEX. Education degrees typically qualify someone to teach. Civil Engineers are capable of being licensed and practicing as such. As you've probably noticed, these majors tend to be very skill oriented.

2. **Majors leading directly into graduate or professional school**

    This can be any major. Literally, any major. It's all about your intent. If you want to be a biology professor, a bachelor's degree in biology is only the first step in a long journey. You could also major in biology and apply to law school, dental school, med school, MBA programs, and the list goes on. Other majors work the same way. Many universities have joint programs where you'll roll from an undergraduate seamlessly into a graduate program, and, in fact, the two will blend. PharmD (pharmacist) programs are often this way.

3. **Majors leading to a job**

    Again, this can be any major. It's all about your intent. You may have graduate school plans in the future, but want to bolster your apps with a few years of work experience (a good idea for business and law school). Or you may decide "no more classes, no more books." It goes without saying but not every degree qualifies you for every job.

Is There Such a Thing as a Bad Major?

In short, no. Like most choices, every major has its strengths and weaknesses. Those vary based on who you are, what your goals are, and what school you attend has its own considerations (there *are* strong programs and weak programs).

There can be bad majors for you. Some majors may be too easy (you aren't challenging yourself). Some majors may be too demanding or a poor fit for your temperament, interests, and academic abilities (do not use that as an excuse not to try).

There can be bad departments at your school. The strength of the department will affect the quality of your education and, equally important, affect the opportunities you have for internships, research, employment, and graduate school placement. You should also look at what clubs, activities, pre-professional societies the department offers.

Can your major/department help you reach your goal? If you want to work as an investment banker in New York, you need to find a business school where banks recruit. In all industries, relationships between the college/university and employers are incredibly important—as are the alumni connections.

What is the industry like? Some industries, like fashion merchandising or entertainment (acting/film/music) are tournament industries. In tournament industries, a few people at the top make most of the money. These are highly competitive industries and your alma mater may make a ton of difference or no difference at all. Do what your heart tells you, but if you major in drama, be prepared to wait tables.

A Note About STEM

Education has fads and trends like anything else. For the years you've been in school, STEM has been chief among those fads. I don't mean that Science, Technology, Engineering, and Mathematics are fads, nor do I think that their importance has been overblown in your education (I think STEM is awesome). I have noticed, however, that a mythos has been built around the economics of having a STEM degree.

Not all STEM degrees are created equal in terms of employment, career trajectory and earnings. For the most part, STEM degrees pay more than less technical degrees, but a B.S. in Biology will generally pay less than an Engineering degree and the biology major is much more likely to be underemployed.

Many STEM degrees are the first step in an educaiton. For life science majors—biology, chemistry, and related fields—the end goal is often professional school in medicine. If that's the case, the earning differential at the undergraduate level doesn't matter. I will caution you, however, a Ph.D. in a science offers no guarantees. The US and other countries produce far more science Ph.D.'s than we can actually use.

Colleges are hiring fewer full-time, tenure-track faculty and, instead, paying adjuncts and lecturers almost nothing to shoulder the load (a despicable practice for both the would-be-professors and students). The private sector, unfortunately, can't absorb all of the excess, and it's becoming increasingly common for newly minted Ph.D.'s to take post-doctoral fellowships for lack of other opportunities.

Choosing a Major

Between 20 and 50% of students enter college undecided. At some schools, there are exploratory tracks or meta-majors, to allow you to explore a cluster of related disciplines all while keeping you on track to graduate. At most schools, however, you're on your own. It's also highly likely you'll change majors, 75 – 80% of students do. (Check out the chapter on *Changing Majors* for more). Here's my advice for picking a major.

Don't be in a rush. There's no correlation between having a major declared in your first semester or first year and graduation rate. In fact, you're less likely (according to one study) to graduate or graduate on time, if you stick with a major that doesn't fit you. But, you do have to make a decision. Some colleges require you to declare by the end of your first year, some the second year. You need to have a pretty good idea of a major by the end of fall your sophomore year and have a decision by the end of that year. Otherwise, you run a very high risk of extending your graduation date.

I'm breaking majors down in two ways: how you plan to use the major (you just read that part) and how certain you are in your choice of major. Don't expect to fit perfectly within either set of categories, but they can be useful in helping you think through your situation. Everyone is different; we all have our strengths, weaknesses, hopes, and fears.

I Know What I Want to Do

A small percentage of you have known you want to be an engineer, doctor, or accountant since before you darkened Kindergarten's door. If that's you, awesome. There's nothing wrong with knowing what you want and going after it. I will say this, however, don't be afraid to explore other disciplines, and make sure this is what *you* really want. If you discover that your expectations are wildly different from the reality, or if another field enthralls you, don't be afraid to change.

It's really important to your happiness and success that you're the one who wants to be a doctor, lawyer, engineer, or whatever. If you do not want that, have a difficult conversation with whomever in your life is pushing you in that direction. It's better for them, and it's far better for you in the end. If you don't want that future, it's likely you'll never get there, and you'll be miserable the whole way to failure. Even worse, you may get there and feel trapped in a life you didn't want for yourself.

I Think I Know What I Want to Do

If you know you want to "do something in medicine," or "attend business or law school" you likely fall into this category. You've narrowed things down to a domain, and you're waiting to see how your abilities and interests line up with potential graduate education/career prospects. Don't be afraid to do a 180° if reality doesn't meet your expectations.

Depending on your final career goal, your major can be pretty flexible. You can major in a lot of things and go on to medical school, dental school, PT school, law school, etc. Stay on track with your general electives and explore related disciplines. You won't waste any credits once you declare.

If you're considering a skill-based degree like accounting, nursing, or engineering, you'll need to take a few classes in that discipline so you don't fall behind. Taking those classes will also help you decide whether the class is for you. Later, if you decide to go a different direction, those credits will fill general education requirements.

I Have No Clue What I Want to Do

If you're in this group, you're in a better place than you think. You are more likely to look at your courses as a Tinder date to a discipline, and that will keep you engaged (a lot of the time, at least) in your classes. The world is wide open and not being sure is a great way to find a major for the *right* reasons.

I strongly suggest you take some courses that you wouldn't take normally. Look at it this way; you've been taking English comp, life sciences, math, US/World History, and so on for your entire life. Try some things you've never been exposed to.

Shouldn't I Pick the Major that Makes Most Money?

Johnny Cash said that being rich meant, "…having to worry about every damn thing in the world except money." The Man in Black was right on that one. I have been poor, and I can tell you that a chronic lack of money adds a tremendous amount of stress and negative emotions like hopelessness, sadness, regret, and anger.

But above a certain threshold, you've just removed one thing from the "worry" list. If you don't trust me or a dead country music legend, trust the research. Negative emotions start to dissipate when you have a household income of about $70,000. At $160,000, those feelings almost entirely gone. Above $200,000, extra money doesn't result in fewer negative feelings or reduced happiness. That's a household income (two adults working and supporting some kids). **For individuals, incomes above $75,000 don't result in any additional happiness.**

You're going to be working for a *long* time, probably more than twice as long as you've been alive. You need to find something that you're passionate about and that you're good at. The people who are most successful aren't the brightest or most ambitious; they are the people who have found the right fit. You'll be happier, healthier, and more successful by finding something that fits you, and you will have the best chance of living a satisfied life and changing the world along the way.

Money is Important

It is important to make enough money to survive. After you enter the workforce, whether it's with an undergraduate or graduate degree, you want to be able to make enough to live, pay on your student loans, and hopefully save.

There are two issues to consider: how much do jobs in that field pay, and how hard is it to find work in that field. On one end of the spectrum, you have petroleum engineering, where recent college grads can often find salaries around, or even exceeding $100,000 a year, and unemployment is—usually—quite low. On the other hand, you have library science graduates who have a low median wage throughout their career and a high unemployment rate.

There's no strong correlation between job stability and pay. Nurses make somewhat more than the average college grad and have very little unemployment. Teachers also have very little unemployment, but they make somewhat less than the average college grad. Some majors, most notably the dramatic arts, are chronically underemployed—doing jobs that don't require a college education.

Don't just look at the "sticker salary." The average salary (by the way, median is a much better measure of what people earn) isn't very informative. Research how stable the industry/field is, how automation and AI may affect traditional jobs in that industry, what the field's growth rate is expected to be over the next 10 and 20 years, the distribution and range of earnings, what percentage of people are unemployed or underemployed, and so on.

Life is about tradeoffs. For many of you, you'll have to decide how much stability you want to trade for passion. I lean more towards passion, so long as it's very realistic for you to build a stable financial life. But, I don't know your answer. I encourage you to think hard about it, not just now, but throughout your life. You can always change directions.

Should I Double Major?

Some double majors are clearly advantageous (like pairing two types of engineering, or engineering and chemistry). **For most disciplines, however, a double major is unlikely to give you a competitive advantage in getting a job.**

Somewhat paradoxically, there is a bump in earnings for double majors, but I wouldn't necessarily argue that the bump is caused by the double major. It may be that individuals who are willing to take on two majors are also more likely to be more ambitious and willing to work harder. In the Resources section of the chapter, I've listed an excellent article that exams data on double majoring to help you decide what's best for you. Here's what I would weigh when considering a double major:

Can you still finish in four years? If you're taking out some serious student loans, the extra semester or year is adding quite a bit to your debt. The same is true if you have to take summer classes.

What will you be giving up? If you're stuck taking multiple summer classes every year, you'll be missing out on internships, research projects, and study abroad opportunities. Being a well-rounded, impactful person is important on graduate and professional school applications. Internship and out-of-class experience is incredibly important for those students trying to launch a career after earning their undergraduate degree. Double majoring will also severely restrict the courses you can take, as you'll be plenty busy trying to fulfill the requirements of both majors.

All that said, if you feel like you should do it, then by all means do it.

Staying on Track to Graduate in 4

Because the major constitutes the most specific training in your undergraduate education, it has the most hierarchy (class A has to be taken before class B). A small error in scheduling can knock you off track to graduate in time. Here are some guidelines.

1. **Plan ahead**. Your advisor or department will have some sort of checklist available with all the courses you'll need to graduate. Make yourself a flowchart, if necessary, to follow the prerequisites up the chain. Discuss your understanding with your advisor to make sure you're both on the same page. If your major has pre-req's that will block your progress, make sure you get those out of the way as soon as possible (see the next item). Try and leave yourself an extra semester on your major courses, that way if you miss a pre-req or have to repeat a course, there's breathing room.

    I know the planning step seems a little obvious or silly, but a lack of planning prevents thousands of students from graduating each year.

2. **Watch out for bottlenecks.** Important courses, or sequences of courses, may only be offered one time per year. If you miss your chance, you'll hit a wall on your major until the next time you can take the course. For example, if you're a chem major, or a biochem major, organic chemistry is a pre-req to a lot of higher division courses. If the two-course sequence is only offered once a year starting in the fall, you cannot miss taking it.

3. **Prioritize.** Your major work should come first, particularly in courses that are important pre-requisites or bottlenecks. You'll be so much better off if you get through those courses the first time.

4. **Don't forget you need to take other classes.** I fell into this trap. I neglected to take a couple of general education classes until the fall of my senior year. Had I not remembered, I may have had to add a semester. While your major defines your degree, you have to complete the general education requirements to graduate. (They're important too, check out the chapter on *General Education*).

189

Minors

Minors offer you the option of getting somewhat deeper into a discipline, but without the burden of fulfilling all the requirements of a major. Again, they're typically not that useful in getting a job and don't necessarily do much for a grad/professional school application. Your department may require you to complete a minor. This is more likely for majors in the social sciences and humanities.

Resources

The Economic Guide to Picking a College Major Ben Casselman	fivethirtyeight.com/features/the-economic-guide-to-picking-a-college-major/
Majors & Happiness.... Michael Edmondson	thecollege.syr.edu/-pdfs-docs/career-pdfs/Major%20in%20Happiness.pdf
Does it Pay to Double Major Christos Makridis	pbs.org/newshour/economy/pay-get-double-major-college

32 CHANGING MAJORS

You've almost certainly been told, "don't change your major if you want to graduate in four years." It's well-intentioned but, like all advice, it's not true in all situations. To be honest, telling you not to change your major is a waste of time. The vast majority of you will change your major at some point.

You know what? **I don't mind if you change your major as long as it's for the right reasons.** College should be about exploration, and if you're a traditional student, you grow and change quite a bit from 17 or 18 to 21 or 22 years old. If you're a nontraditional student, you're still being exposed to new ideas, disciplines, and are considering wholly different careers. In fact, one sizeable study found that students who changed their major at least once were slightly more likely to graduate. Please read the section at the end of this chapter titled *Reasons for Changing Majors*.

But I don't want your change of major to delay your graduation. And I know you don't want that either. Here's how to change your major without changing your graduation date.

When & To What

How a change in major will affect your potential graduation date is an issue of when you decide to change majors and what you decide to change to.

When – If you change majors in the first two years, up until junior year, most students don't lose credits and are able to make up the modest amount of major work that would have been done by that point. That's because, of course, your first two years is typically loaded with the general electives and prerequisites for your major courses. Furthermore, it's likely, since you're switching to that major, that you've had at least the introductory course in that subject.

191

To What – The closer your major is to the one you're leaving, the more overlap there will be. For example, a switch from biology to biochemistry or from accounting to finance, won't cost credits unless you're very far along.

The closer your current major is to the one you're considering, the farther along you can be in your studies without a major change setting you back. In fact, one study found that 25% of students who switched majors in their sixth term (conventionally speaking the spring of junior year) still graduated on time. It's likely that most of these students were switching to closely related majors.

Switching out of STEM is common. and the credits you've earned will cover many of the thornier general education requirements. Switching into STEM (less common, but worthwhile) can be trickier, particularly in disciplines like engineering where you'll have a two semester sequence on "Principles of Engineering" that has to be completed before any other coursework. In general, switching to a technical discipline from a non-technical discipline is more likely to extend your graduation date.

Long story short, if you're changing before your junior year, there's a good chance you can catch up to graduate in four years. If you're changing between closely related majors, you make it easier.

Why are You Changing Majors?

Put some serious self-examination into why you're changing majors. There are some problems that you can't resolve by changing your educational "locale" because, guess what, wherever you are there you'll be.

I can't cut it. There's a line around the block at the advising center right after the first test of the semester is given. Everyone has suddenly had the realization that they don't want to be a doctor, engineer, or mathematician. Before you jump to that conclusion and give up at the first hurdle, exhaust the other options available to you. Please check out the chapters on *Tests, Quizzes, & Assignments* for more information on resources available to you, how to set goals, and how to study.

In all honesty, it's possible your current major isn't for you. But you owe yourself the chance to try. You won't be wasting any time, you can use those credits to fill out some general education requirements, and if you get through the first few series of courses, then you are capable of earning the degree (in almost all cases). If you don't believe me on the last one, ask one of your professors.

I hate it. Do you hate it or is it hard? Those are different things. If it's hard, you need to ask yourself if it's worth it. If you hate it, have no interest in it, and find yourself disconnecting from your education, then switch majors.

It's not what I thought. That's a pretty common feeling, and it can be a valid reason for changing majors. Remember that the jobs your current major leads to are going to be very different from the education in class. Also, upper division courses tend to be much different from the intro level stuff. Talk to a professor or your advisor, if they're in the department, about how what you're experiencing isn't like what you expected. I'd also encourage you to check out related disciplines because something drew you to that major in the first place. For example, it may be that you thought you loved psychology but you're really into social work.

It won't get me where I want to be. This is a legitimate concern and it may not be solved by changing majors (check out the chapter on *Transferring Colleges* for more). I will say this, however, the way is usually broader than people think. It's easy, especially when we're stressed, to see only one potential path to where we're sure we need to be. That line of thinking results in a vision of the future that seems very fragile. Talk to someone, advisor or professor, in the department. Explain what you want, and they'll tell you how, or if they can, help you get there.

Look Before You Leap

Usually a change in major means that you're unhappy, uncomfortable, or both. When we feel like that, we're usually more focused on the "getting out" than the where we'll "get in." This can be problematic. **Before you do anything, talk to a professor in the department, your adviser, and then weigh your options.**

33 ADVISING

Without question, advising is one of the most important aspects of college. It's also a task that students tend to blow off or rush through. Don't. **A good advisor can add a lot of value by helping you find opportunities, suggest courses, identify scholarships, and provide a letter of recommendation. Most of all, a good advisor will help keep you on track to graduate in four years**.

Be an Informed Consumer

For most of you, your education is the first major purchase you've made in adulthood. Know what you want out of it, and use your advisor to help you reach your goals.

How to be an Informed Consumer

1. **Set Goals –** You need to have goals for your semester, your time in undergrad, and your career. If you're undecided, a good career goal is "keeping your options open."

2. **Do Your Homework –** Know what you need for your major, and research what you should take that will benefit your major. Look into professors, course options, and timetables. Don't forget to take time to explore the "dark corners" of the course catalog to find courses that pique your interest.

3. **Ask Advice & Listen –** There are plenty of students who go to their advising appointment with a very specific idea of what they want. Knowing what you want is great, but do ask—and listen to—your adviser's opinion. Remind him or her of your longer-term goals and ask what they recommend. Ask about extracurricular

activities and other opportunities that fit your interests and objectives.

4. **Advisers Respond, They do not Initiate** – The burden is on you to contact your adviser and come prepared with good questions and plans. At some colleges, you may be required to meet with your adviser 6 or more times your first year, but you'll set the appointments.

Types of Advisers

Undergraduate Advising Centers – Professional advisers, not faculty members, advise undergraduates, typically freshmen and sophomores. Another version of this is the "first-year adviser" or "freshman adviser" who works with students for the first year before they transition to a departmental adviser. First year/freshmen advising programs tend to be more holistic, addressing issues like time management and organization, and they may also be tied into the college/university's orientation course.

To be frank, the quality of undergraduate advising centers is pretty variable. The same, however, can be said of departmental advisers. Make sure you come prepared with your goals. If you want to study abroad, for example, bring it up right away; your adviser can help you get set up to make study abroad a reality.

Don't worry overmuch that your adviser could accidentally send you down the wrong track. The couple years of college is filled with a lot of general education courses and pre-requisites, so it's very unlikely you'll be set back in any meaningful way.

Departmental Advisers – Departmental advisers are faculty members within the department. They may be a professor or a lecturer. To my knowledge, no college uses adjunct instructors and many require faculty to be on tenure-track. Your adviser has the advantage of being intimately familiar with your department and the requirements you'll need to satisfy for graduation. They may relish working with undergraduate advisees, or they may look at it as an unfortunate part of their job.

As with any adviser, be clear about your post-college objectives, insomuch

195

as you can. Also, make sure you tell your adviser about any goals that lay outside the department (something like study abroad).

Departmental advisors have unmatched familiarity with the department and its workings and associations in industry and at other institutions. As such, departmental advisers can be particularly helpful in recommending extracurricular activities, helping you find undergraduate internships and research opportunities, and writing you letters of recommendation. As such, the relationship with your adviser is of paramount importance.

Your Relationship with Your Advisor

Just like your relationships with professors, the relationship with your adviser is based on professionalism. Keep your appointments, come prepared, write professional emails, and address your adviser appropriately.

The better you know your adviser and the better your adviser knows you, the better off you'll be.

Guidelines for Building a Relationship with Your Advisor

1. **Follow the Golden Rule.** Treat your advisor the way you'd have your advisor treat you. Respond promptly, be on time and be prepared, be polite, and take an interest in them.

2. **You want your adviser to know you.** Relationships are built on reciprocity. You want your adviser to know you? Then know your adviser. relationship with you, it needs to be <u>appropriately</u> personal. Ask about them. Where did they go to school? What got them interested in their discipline?

3. **Make the relationship multidimensional.** Take at least one of their courses, particularly if you'd like to use them as a reference or for a letter of recommendation. Understand their research focus and maybe even read a few of their publications.

Approaching a Professor as Adviser

At most colleges, your departmental advisor will be selected for you. At some schools, particularly if you're a member of the honor's college, you may have an option. Remember, full professors and department chairs may have very few (or no) undergraduate advising slots. You should approach someone whose class you enjoyed, studies something you're interested in, has a reputation for taking undergraduate advising seriously, and/or you believe will help you achieve your goals in some other way.

I recommend that you ask in person during office hours, during a pre-arranged meeting (email and schedule). I would introduce why you'd like them to be your advisor, particularly citing how you liked some specific details about their course or research. Then ask if they would be willing to take you on.

They may say no. Advisees are a significant time commitment, and they only have so much time or so many slots. If they say no, ask them who they would recommend.

Your First Advising Appointment

Balance Your Load – Try and take one course from your major (or from a potential major), one course that you won't want to take later, one course that you need for your potential major, and a course where you can explore a new field while also fulfilling a general education requirement. Make sure that you feel confident with at least one course and ask your advisor about the workload for other courses you are considering. You don't want to have too much of one type of work—insomuch as that's avoidable—so balance between courses that involve more problem solving and those that involve more reading, more papers versus more tests and so on.

Take the Orientation Course – Almost all colleges offer a course on how to succeed at that school. It may be graded or pass/fail, and the courses range between 1 – 3 credits. It's almost always required, but take it even if it's optional.

Subsequent Advising Appointments

Be Proactive – Advisers aren't just for registration. If you're struggling for personal or professional (word choice) reasons, go and speak to your adviser. They will likely give you some helpful direction on how to overcome your current adversity, help you access campus resources, and give you invaluable feedback on dealing with your professors during this time. *Also be proactive about signing up for your advising appointment; the sooner you signup and register the more likely you are to get the courses you want/need.*

Evaluate Your Goals – Have your college/career goals changed? If so, make your adviser aware. Also, discuss any potential change in goals with your adviser (more on that in the next pages).

Do Your Homework – Advising isn't just about the semester/quarter that you're enrolling for, look ahead. Many classes are only offered in one term; if you want those classes you'll want to register for them when they are available, and knock out any pre-req's beforehand.

Don't Overburden Yourself – Students who have performed well often want to amp up the difficulty of their next term. There's nothing wrong with that, but use some discretion and pay attention to what else is going on in your life. If you're a junior applying to professional school in the fall, you'll have to manage your courses as well as preparing for your GRE, GMAT, LSAT, MCAT, PCAT, or DAT.

Make Sure You're on Track – Make sure that you're getting the courses you need to graduate on time. Be especially careful if you go to a smaller schools where there are fewer sections of courses and many courses will only be taught once a year.

Ask About Scholarships – Scholarships aren't only for incoming freshmen; ask if there are any departmental or university scholarships for current students. Don't be deterred if the scholarship amounts are somewhat lower. Not only does every bit help (check out the chapter on *Financial Aid* for more), but these scholarships are great additions to a resume. Often, these scholarships are less competitive because of lack of interest.

Ask About Opportunities – Your adviser can be an excellent resource for finding internships, research opportunities, study abroad experiences, and eventually jobs. Do some research, both online and by asking other students within your department, but make sure you ask if there's anything you missed.

Change in Major or Change in Goals

Explain the rationale for changing – If you are considering changing your major, or your career goals have changed, schedule an appointment with your adviser ASAP. At that appointment, openly and honestly discuss why you're changing plans.

Ask your adviser their honest opinion – Depending on how well your adviser knows you, they may point out where your reasoning could be clouded or in error.

That said, they are advisers, so your academic career is in your hands.

Consider their advice – Don't make any decisions right away. If you've been in college for awhile, you run the risk of losing a bunch of hours by changing majors. If you're new to college, remember that you're still adjusting and that college is difficult at first.

Get a second opinion – If you're changing majors drastically, say going from English to Biology, I recommend that you talk to another adviser to make sure you have a clear idea of how this will affect your timeline for graduation. You can do this with a departmental adviser from the major you're thinking of switching to or with an adviser from an undergraduate/first year advising center.

Meet again with your adviser – If you decide to move ahead, meet one more time with your current advisers. If, on the other hand, you decide to stick with your major/goal, meet again with your adviser to explain why you decided to stick it out.

If you're changing majors or goals, don't feel awkward about telling your adviser so. They won't take it personally, and they want the best for you. In a lot of ways, professors remember what students tend to forget: college is a time for exploration.

Bad Advisers

Much is written about what to do if you have a bad adviser at the graduate level. That relationship is a lot more complex and your adviser has a lot more power over you than your undergraduate adviser. But, a bad undergraduate adviser can be a nightmare that costs you opportunities, makes life tougher, and could add thousands of dollars to the cost of your degree. Bad advisers are uninterested, unknowledgeable, unorganized, and/or unorganized. It's unlikely you can change your adviser's behavior, so think about what you can take and what you can't.

Let's be clear on what advisers should do. A good undergraduate adviser keeps you on track to graduate, makes specific recommendations based on their knowledge of you, identifies opportunities for you, and thinks about your academic career more than one semester at a time. Advisers aren't there to push you all the way to a cap and gown, nor are they there to plan your life for you.

If your adviser isn't great, it's even more important that you're an informed consumer. If you can't deal with the adviser, consider requesting a change.

Changing Advisers

The procedure for changing advisers varies quite a bit, and it may be different depending on whether you have a faculty adviser or professional adviser in an advising center.

In general, you have to file some sort of form requesting the change. If you're going from faculty-to-faculty or from advising center to faculty, make sure that whomever you plan to switch to can take you on. At some colleges, you may want have to meet with a dean or department chair to discuss your change.

Be polite and positive about why you're changing. It's OK to point out difficulties you've had, but don't be vitriolic or wholly negative. This is particularly important if you're changing from a departmental adviser and you aren't changing majors.

34 BAD TEST, BAD CLASS, BAD SEMESTER

Bad things will happen to you in life. They happen to me, they happen to everyone, and I wouldn't have it any other way. Don't get me wrong, I don't enjoy them, but **they keep you humble, hungry, and allow you to problem solve in a way that success never can**. For many of you, you're first real catastrophe will happen in college.

First, I want you to consider how you're defining failure. If it's an A- on an exam, you ought to think again. If you don't have concrete definitions of failure and success, almost all of your efforts will be failures. I urge you to read the section on perfectionism in the chapter *Building Your Academic Life*.

I know some of you are reading this before it applies, but most of you are reading this because something bad happened. Whatever disaster you're currently experiencing is a great opportunity (although I know it doesn't feel like it). **Resilience, the ability to bounce back, is the most important trait you can have. Failure is not final and it is not unacceptable: failure is part of life.**

Key Components of Resilience

1. **Resilience does not mean you're not upset or distressed**.
2. **Resilience requires commitment to your success and your goals.**
3. **Resilience requires you to focus on what you can control vs. what you cannot.** People who focus their efforts and thoughts on what they can control have a stronger sense of agency.
4. **Resilience requires you to feel good about yourself and manage intense feelings and impulses.**
5. **Resilience requires the ability to make realistic plans and work towards executing them.**

Build Your Resilience

Resilience is a developed skill, not an innate trait. Your personal response to tough times will vary—everyone reacts to terrible news in his or her own way. But after the immediate response, you can take steps to turn the awful into a learning experience.

1. **Develop Awareness –** You need to figure out what your primary stressors are in life and how your behavior changes when you feel stress. Do you make healthy lifestyle choices? Do you have physical symptoms like tension headaches? Do you have sleep disturbances? Do you dwell on the stressor or find yourself unable to focus on anything?

2. **Examine Your Thoughts –** For many people, worries about the future are considerable stressors. Ask yourself if you're thinking rationally. How much control do you have over future events? How likely are the terrible outcomes you imagine? Watch out for generalizing a specific outcome, for example, you're not a failure just because you failed a biology exam.

3. **It's Practice not Performance –** Treat everything in life as if it's a rehearsal. It will help keep you from the perfectionist mindset, and it will open you up to learning from mistakes as you—like everyone—inevitably make them.

4. **Define Your Purpose** – Understanding how things fit in your goal system will allow you to see what's in front of you as one step on a long path. It will also make you more optimistic.

5. **Believe** – You need to hope that things will get better. This doesn't mean go buy a bunch of scratch-off lottery tickets, instead, you should focus on *believing that you will make things better*. Identify actionable steps that you can take to move forward. Damn the torpedoes, full speed ahead.

6. **A Solid Support Network** – Surround yourself with goal-oriented people. You'll work harder, receive more actionable advice, and stay more motivated. The key is finding people who take ownership of their lives and developing your relationship with them.

Bad Test/Paper/Assignment/Project

Feel Bad for a Minute – It's entirely appropriate to feel bad about a bad grade. But cap your grief. Give yourself an hour or even a day—but no longer—and then move into proactive mode. Being sad, angry, or both for longer won't change the grade, but it could hurt your grades going forward.

Put the Failure in Perspective – Run the numbers. See how this affects what you can get in the course, and how you'll have to do to make up for it. It may be a little, or it may be quite a bit. If you figure out that you're stuck with a low grade at best, remember that this is one course out of approximately 40 that you'll take.

What Does it Mean – In the broader scheme of you graduating in four years and moving on to a career or graduate school, what does this course mean? Is it an important course for your major progression, are the skills in this course foundational for others you'll be taking, or is it less integral to your progression to your major?

See Your Professor – Always see your professor if you've gotten a bad grade on a significant assignment or assessment. Don't argue about your grade, instead, ask about how you can do better. For more specific advice check out the chapters on *Dealing with Professors*.

Determine What Happened – You should figure out, in a concrete way, what went wrong. Did you start studying too late, study too little, miss too many classes, or have the wrong approach?

Make a Plan for Next Time – It is absolutely vital that you make a concrete plan, broken into actionable steps, on how to avoid this the next time around. Use the resources provided by your professor and the college. Set a study schedule. Use good time management techniques. Check out the chapters on *Organization, Time Management,* & *Study Habits* for more.

Bad Course

Before Things Get too Bad – Don't just pay attention to your grades. Keep an eye on how you're doing and feeling during class; if you're feeling lost or having difficulty keeping up with the workload, that problem will only get worse unless it is addressed. As soon as you feel yourself struggling, it's time to see your professor.

See Your Professor – Explain the nature of your difficulties and ask for advice. Professors are happy to help you, but they are unlikely to change the format of their course to make your life easier. Going to office hours also indicates to the professor that you are serious about their course and proactive about your education.

Dropping a Class – Every college has drop dates, usually right after the middle of the term. **Make sure you see your professor before you drop**. Dropped classes show up on your transcript, and while a few are OK, you don't want a bunch nor do you want to get yourself in the habit of giving up.

Also, if the course is required, you may be best off finishing out the course and doing your best, even if there's a low likelihood you'll pass. Most colleges offer D/F repeats during your first two years (or 60 hours). If you can take a D/F repeat, your better grade will replace your initial grade.

In cases where you find the subject material particularly difficult, or the course is cumulative, many students benefit from going through the course first. All too often, someone will drop a tough course (college algebra for example) only to retake it the following semester. They do well in their second run at the course until they hit the material that came after the drop.

Put it in Perspective – This is one course in a series of about ~40 courses that you'll take as you earn your degree. One course will not keep you from being a doctor, lawyer, professor, physical therapist, consultant, etc.

Determine What Happened – You may need a day or a few days to be able to look at the situation rationally (do keep a cap on the mourning though). Something went wrong, and you'll need to figure out what it is so you can avoid making the same mistake in the future. Speak to your professor again and focus on being proactive about another attempt at that course or similar courses.

Evaluate Your Options – Do you plan to retake the course? If so, your plan will focus on how to succeed in that course.

Make a Plan – If necessary, change your next semester's schedule to make it easier to devote more time to the course. You may also want to consider changing professors. Most important, though, are the changes you need to make to how you're working on the class.

Bad Semester

Before Things Get too Bad – What's happening? Seriously, if all of your courses are going poorly, and this hasn't happened to you in the past, there must be some issue. Do you have an external event or maybe some internal issue that are affecting your performance? Are you unhappy and engaging in some sort of subconscious rebellion? Look to yourself, and try to make

Put it in Perspective – I promise you that one semester won't ruin your dreams, and I assure you that you're not the first person to have had a terrible semester.

Talk to Your Adviser – Please get an outside opinion on what's going on academically. Your adviser knows more than you think, and may have incredibly useful advice. I also strongly urge you to talk to a counselor.

Determine What Happened – People are complicated. There's probably more than one cause for your predicament. Don't be reductive, and put all the blame on one aspect of your life. Similarly, don't buy into overly simple solutions. Being "tougher" and "working harder" are not actionable solutions.

Make a Plan – One semester won't ruin your ambitions, but multiple bad semesters will. Your job is to prevent this from happening again. Figure out how to balance your life, take care of yourself, be happy, and be an effective student. You've got to be a well balanced person to succeed in the long-run; take this opportunity to address any aspects of life you've been ignoring.

35 TRANSFERRING COLLEGES

Unfortunately, transferring colleges has become epidemic, over one-third of students transfer colleges prior to graduating or dropping out. **Transferring is one of the most common reasons that students do not graduate in four years.**

The most common transfer type is students transferring from 4-year institutions to community colleges. It should be the other way around. 40% of college students study at a community college, and the vast majority of those students have the goal of earning a baccalaureate degree, which community colleges do not offer.

Do not transfer unless you have clear and compelling reasons. Seriously evaluate whether changing schools will make a substantial difference. Be patient with where you are now, and explore less extreme options. If you're unhappy, transferring may not solve the problem. After all, wherever you go, it'll still you in the mirror.

From a practical standpoint, students are increasingly likely to pursue a transfer to reduce tuition and living costs, enter a higher quality program or a program that provides more opportunities for their goals, or to transfer to a better "name brand".

Why Are You Transferring?

People transfer for a lot of reasons logistical, financial, emotional, goal-oriented. I'm not telling you to transfer or not to transfer, but I do want to take a look at some of the reasons people transfer.

Matriculate to Four Year Institution – Community college students who have the goal of obtaining a Bachelor's degree *will have to transfer.*

What to Look Out For – Be proactive, as soon as you enroll in community college, check to see if they have transfer agreements with four-year schools. Transfer agreements will allow you to keep most or all of your hours and may guarantee admission, provided you have a certain GPA and number of hours.

Money – Circumstances have changed, or you've started to realize how much debt you're piling on. You may also have decided that *current college X* doesn't give you any more opportunity than the somewhat less expensive *future college Y.*

What to Look Out For – See how many of your hours transfer. If you're adding a semester, summer classes, or even a whole year, transferring may cost you money in the end. Also, compare cost of living.

Program Strength/Availability – Not every college/university has every program. If you started in civil engineering, but then decided your passion was landscape architecture, then you'll have to transfer. Alternatively, you may decide on or change majors and want to transfer to a school with a stronger programs.

What to Look Out For – Again, pay attention to how much transferring will cost, both in terms of lost credits, higher tuition, lost scholarships, lost financial aid, and/or cost of living. Program rankings are somewhat arbitrary, and going from 50th to 40th probably won't do much for you. Really research the differences between your existing program and your transfer program. Find out what extracurricular activities and opportunities they offer. Research what happens to graduates, in terms of employment and/or graduate school admission.

Career Opportunities – Pay attention to what employers are represented at career fairs at your current school and the school you are considering. Research those employers. If you're pre-professional or planning on graduate studies, check where recent graduates have matriculated and find out which graduate/professional schools come to campus.

For example, you may have decided to be an investment banker. Ideally, you'd want to attend a business program that has a strong history of sending students to superday interviews at banks, has banks and other financial institutions come to campus, and has a strong alumni network in that field. I worked with a young man once who had transferred from the University of Maryland, which has a very strong business school, to the much more expensive New York University. He believed that the location and opportunities at NYU was worth the additional cost.

<u>What to Look Out For</u> – Beware of falling into the grass is greener fallacy. You need to do your homework and really figure out what opportunities are available to at *current college x* versus *future college y*. If you work hard and advocate for yourself, you can create some amazing opportunities at whatever school you're at.

Prestige/Brand – I won't lie, prestige is important, regardless of whether you plan to go straight into a career or attend graduate/professional school. More prestigious schools have more money, better alumni networks, and generally more opportunities.

<u>What to Look Out For</u> – I think this can be a significant factor in your decision to transfer, but I don't like it as the only reason to transfer. You need to have a specific reason other than the grass is greener. It's best to have something specific, a goal or experience you can't achieve or have at your current school. Never transfer because you feel inferior to students from other schools. I've worked with really brilliant people who attended no named colleges and idiots who went to Harvard.

No Longer Playing a Collegiate Sport – So you went to play a sport at your college, but you've drifted away from that sport, got injured, or have changed your focus. This is a pretty good topic for a transfer essay, and it's a very valid reason to transfer. If you were injured or otherwise lost your athletic scholarship, there's financial inducement as well. I've had particularly good luck counseling ex-athletes looking to transfer, as they have a compelling and clear story for transfer.

<u>What to Look Out For</u> – Whether or not you decide to transfer, find some healthy things to fill up your time. You can play intramural, but you may find the competition level leaves something to be desired. As a college athlete, you were very busy, make sure you funnel that extra time, energy, and competitiveness into healthy pursuits that line up with your personal

and professional goals. Play close attention to the financial end. If you've lost some academic scholarship, go to financial aid and see what they can do. They're likely to help you if they know you'll have to transfer otherwise.

Be Close to Home – You can have very valid reasons for transferring to a college/university closer to home. A change in family situation, like a sick parent or sibling could make moving closer necessary. Similarly, a change in financial status, financial aid status, or a desire to save money by living at home can also make sense. That said, the overwhelming majority of students who transfer to be closer to home do so for the wrong reasons.

<u>What to Look Out For</u> – If you are moving home because you are homesick, or have had trouble adjusting, I encourage you to hold off. This is a big moment in your life, and it can be terrifying for some. It is, however, a great opportunity to learn that you are more adaptable than you think you are. The more extreme version is moving home to be with a high school boyfriend/girlfriend. Please do not do that. Check out the section on homesickness in the chapter *Building Your Life* for more.

Not the Right Fit – You may go to a school that just doesn't fit you. Your peers don't have similar goals, are too serious and competitive or vice versa, the academic standards seem too loose or overly intimidating. This is a valid reason to transfer, but be patient with your school.

<u>What to Look Out For</u> – Is it not the right fit, or are you homesick? Could you challenge yourself more, or redistribute challenges to make your path easier? Are you having trouble dealing with the academic demands, self-starting, or organizing yourself? Are you having trouble meeting people and finding a core group of friends? Are you having roommate issues? If you were physically active in high school, have you stopped exercising?

Be brutally honest in your assessment. For more on dealing with these issues, check out the following chapters *Building a Happy Life*; *Meeting People*; *Getting Involved*; *Roommates*; and *Eat, Sleep, Exercise*.

How Transferring Works

Here's what you'll have to do:

1. Fill out an application
2. Send a copy of your college transcript

Depending on where you hope to transfer, the application step could also include:

1. High school transcript
2. An admissions essay or essays[*]
3. Obtain letters of recommendation from professors
4. Have an interview with an admissions officer
5. Submit ACT/SAT scores[#]

How Colleges Evaluate Transfer Applications

The application process is different than applying as a freshman. Here are the differences:

Your college transcript is the biggest factor. Your GPA needs to be high, very high if you're trying to move to a more selective school. It's not just the GPA though, you'll need to take a rigorous course load. If you're transferring with a specific program in mind, take courses that challenge you and are appropriate for your stated goals.

Your high school GPA and SAT/ACT score matter less. In general, the more time since high school, the less your high school GPA and SAT/ACT score matter. Colleges recognize people change and view long ago test dates and grades as old data. You may want to consider retaking the SAT/ACT if you're applying to competitive schools.

Your essay demonstrates your seriousness and rationale. You need to be positive, concrete, and forward-looking in your essay. You need to show

---

[*] Often, these essays ask the question "why do you intend to transfer from your current school to X University?" *Do not* write that essay about what's wrong with your current school. Be positive about your experiences there and the personal growth you've undergone, and how that has led you to the decision to transfer.

[#] Your ACT/SAT score is less important than it was in high school. The more college you've completed and the longer since high school, the less the ACT/SAT matters.

you've done your research on the school you're applying to and particularly the program you want to join. You need to explain why their school fits your plans better than your current school.

Extracurricular activities show time management and campus engagement. Colleges want to see that you're taking advantage of opportunities outside the classroom and adding to the university community. It shows that you can manage time and adds dimensionality to your application. It's also nice if colleges see you participating in some of the same activities you participated in during high school.

Letters of Recommendation from professors attest to your ability, passion, and maturity. Asking for letters can be awkward, particularly if you are using a professor who is also your advisor. (I'm going to talk about the awkwardness of transferring more in the next section). You may have only had intro courses in your major, and, as such, had a huge class size. It's tougher to stand out than it was in high school; you may need to make an impression. Don't skip class, answer questions, get good grades, and go to office hours.

Be honest with the professor about your intentions, don't mislead them. Professors are busy and have a lot of students, so you'll want to meet with your professor after they agree to write the letter to make sure that they'll be able to personalize it appropriately.

You want your professor to know more about you than you got a 95% on your Econ 101 final. In conversations with that professor, stay positive about your current school and your prospective school.

Transferring is Stressful

Aside from restarting the college search and application process, many students find transferring emotionally difficult. If you're transferring for a stronger program, more prestige, or better opportunities, the transfer process can come with a lot of guilt. I've heard it described as a "breakup," and I think this is a fairly accurate description. It can be tough to ask for letters of recommendation because it's implied that "you're just not good enough." Telling friends can be equally difficult.

It's your future, don't let these potentially awkward conversations deter you if, after serious reflection, you've determined transferring is best for you. You have to live your own life.

Transferring Can Be Tough, Depending on the Institution

Overall, transfer acceptances are slightly lower than for freshman admissions. That number varies quite a bit by school, and the college's selectivity in freshmen admissions is a good general indicator of how tough it'll be.

Small colleges/universities typically accept fewer transfer students as they have less room to begin with.

Elite colleges/universities accept very few transfer students. For example, Harvard takes ~12 transfer students a year, less than 1% of the more than 1,600 applicants. Cornell and Penn are more transfer friendly, but admissions percentages are still around the 10% mark.

Larger Universities, particularly state schools, are more likely to be transfer friendly. They've often built out an infrastructure for dealing with transfer students, particularly within their satellite campus system. If a college/university has a transfer coordinator/advisor/department, it's a good sign. These colleges will offer support for transfer students, which may include orientation, courses, or social events.

Financial Aid & Transferring

Just like when you applied as a freshman, you probably won't pay the full "sticker price". Your federal financial aid, so long as you're in good standing, will transfer to your new school. Sallie Mae and Private loans should not be an issue either.

Your Expected Financial Contribution may change, as each school uses the FAFSA differently.

You will lose the merit-based aid (scholarships & grants) your current college and its foundation provide. Any outside scholarships that you've won will have to be transferred over if they are paid to the school directly. You'll need to discuss that issue with your current and future financial aid office. Many of you considering transferring will lose a significant amount in aid.

The good news, you can probably get merit-based aid at your new college.

213

About 80% of colleges/universities offer merit-based aid for transfer students. About two-thirds of medium and large schools offer merit-based aid to transfer students. You may also qualify for other foundation and departmental scholarships.

The bad news, these awards aren't universal, and they tend to be smaller than scholarships you'd get as a freshman. Additionally, these scholarships may only last a year or two, so you may end up coming more out of pocket if it is going to take you longer to finish.

36 TRANSFERRING CREDITS

The advantages of transferring credits in, taking courses under dual enrollment, or receiving credit via AP Test Score are clear. It's a cheap way to get hours and get a leg up before you even arrive on campus.

Transfer/Articulation Agreements

Articulation agreements allow students from a community college to transfer all (or nearly all) of their credits to a four-year college/university that has an agreement with the community college. *Be careful*, maintain a dialogue with both the college/university (they should have transfer admissions counselors) and the community college. You don't want to end up retaking a class, or not getting all of your hours. Transfer Agreements may also guarantee admission for students completing a certain number of hours, or a program, with a specific GPA.

Transferring Hours In

If you're transferring between four-year institutions, how your credits will transfer should be a major consideration as to where/if you'll transfer. The farther along you are in your studies, the more complicated the issue becomes, and you'll want to consult your current college, the prospective college, and the department you'd be transferring to.

If you plan on taking a few classes at a different college to transfer back to your home college, don't make any assumptions. It's very difficult to tell how hours will transfer between institutions. It gets murkier (read: bad news for you) if the course would be part of your major or a major requirement. Make sure you do your homework to save yourself time, money, and frustration. I've said this a few places in the book, but make sure any college you study at, or are thinking about studying at, is accredited and not in danger of losing accreditation. In all cases, your grade in the course will need to be a C or better to transfer the hours.

If you're transferring from a community college to a four-year institution, plan ahead. One reason community college students fail to complete a bachelor's degree is that some, or even all, of their credits don't transfer. According to U.S. News and World Report, the average student transferred with 29.6 credits and <u>lost</u> an average of 12.7 credits—almost half—at their new college/university. Even more astounding, 39.4% of students had 0 hours transfer; they were starting over.[8]

You're more likely to be able to transfer your hours if you stick to general education classes, transfer in-state, and go from a state school to a state school. Do your homework, and avoid wasted time, money, and effort. You may want to consider transferring community colleges if another college has an articulation agreement in place with a four-year college you'd like to attend (most of your hours should transfer from community college to community college). For profit colleges tend to be pretty open to accepting transfer hours, <u>but for-profit colleges are almost always a bad deal for students</u> (see Chapter XX for more).

One last thing, colleges/universities typically require you to complete the last half or third, 52 to 40 hours, give or take, of your credit hours at their institution. Higher-level courses, particularly courses within your major, are unlikely to transfer.

Why is This System So Messed Up?

Money is one reason. Colleges don't make money off of courses you took elsewhere. Also, colleges only get to count you towards their graduation rate if you *started* there. For public colleges/universities, graduation rates are critical for public funding. For public *and* private colleges/universities, graduation rates are a significant component of the ranking game that colleges outwardly protest but inwardly play up to.

AP Tests & Dual Enrollment

Dual Enrollment – Dual enrollment works two ways, and while it's usually

---

[8] https://www.usnews.com/news/national-news/articles/2016-11-22/when-credits-dont-count-transfer-students-face-debt-more-classes

easier to get the credit, your credits will be standard college credits from whomever the dual enrollment agreement is with, and, as such, they may not transfer to your four-year institution. Dual enrollment works two ways:

1. You can take a high school course and earn college credit. Generally, this means taking an AP courses and pay a fee, typically much less than you'd pay for a college class, and receive graded college hours that comport with your course. For example, AP Biology may transfer as Bio 101 & 102.

2. You take a course at a local college, university, or community college and earn high school credit in addition to the college hours. For example, English 101 may count for 11th or 12th grade English.

If your option is to dual enroll at a local community college and your high school offers AP or IB courses, you may be better served by taking the course at your high school (if you're still in the process of applying for colleges). Also, I'm not a huge fan of online classes; in my experience most are not able to faithfully recreate in-person offerings.

AP Tests – Allow you to transfer credits in using your AP Test score (sometimes 3 or above, more commonly 4 or above). If I'm catching you early, i.e. you're still in high school, then always take the AP exams (and prepare for them). You don't have to report the scores on your applications.

One word of caution, If the course has to do with your major, consider retaking the course at your college/university. For example, if you are plan to major in engineering and you squeaked by on your calculus AP exam, or you didn't feel your dual enrollment class was sufficiently challenging, consider retaking Calc 1. You need that solid basis. For that reason, many colleges will allow you to transfer in your credits, but require majors to take a discipline specific introductory course series. You may have gotten a 5 on your AP Bio Exam and receive credit for those hours (Bio 101 & 102) but have to take the major specific intro series of Bio 110 and Bio 111.

217

Placement Tests & Credit by Examination

You'll either be required or have the opportunity to take placement exams that will qualify you for certain courses. This is generally known as credit by examination and if you place out of a course, you'll receive non-graded credit for that course. If you "place out" of a course, for example, Spanish 101, you'll get the three credits on your transcript that aren't graded. Those credits will count toward graduation but they won't affect your GPA.

Credit by examination works great, so long as you aren't putting yourself too far ahead. For example, if you test out of Spanish 101, 102, and 203, you may want to consider starting with Spanish 203 instead of 204. It's up to you, of course, evaluate the decision in terms of your comfort level with that subject and whatever else you have going on that semester.

How Credits Transfer

Your credits won't count towards your GPA (but they will play a major part in an admissions decision, if you are applying as a transfer student, see the previous chapter for more).

Credits can transfer 1 to 1. For example, Econ 101 at your old school becomes Econ 101 at your future alma mater. They also may transfer as unnamed hours if the school doesn't offer that course, or the course you took is significantly different from their same named course. For example, if your British Literature class had different learning objectives, studied different works, and had different themes than the British Literature course at your future college/university, you may end up with three hours of English that have no course number.

Can I Skip Transferring My Hours?

When I get asked this question, it's because your GPA isn't what you'd like it to be. You *may* be able to skate by with that in an employment situation, but graduate/professional schools invariably require you to send transcripts from *all* institutions that you've attended. I guarantee you, if you fail to send a transcript, and they discover it, your offer of admission will be revoked. You don't get much out of not transferring the hours, even if your grades are bad, and you'll be starting from scratch.

FINAL THOUGHTS

Graduating college in four years is a wonderful goal, and I hope you reach it. More than that, I hope you have a wonderful, exciting career full of accolades and accomplishments. Most of all, I hope you build a life that challenges and satisfies you.

11300781R00131

Made in the USA
Lexington, KY
09 October 2018